Service-Learning Code of Ethics

Service-Learning Code of Ethics

Andrea Chapdelaine
Albright College

Ana Ruiz and Judith Warchal
Alvernia College

Carole Wells
Kutztown University

ANKER PUBLISHING COMPANY, INC.
Bolton, Massachusetts

Service-Learning Code of Ethics

ISBN 1-882982-83-5

Composition by Lyn Rodger, Deerfoot Studios
Cover design by Dutton and Sherman Design

ANKER PUBLISHING COMPANY, INC.
563 Main Street
P.O. Box 249
Bolton, MA 01740-0249 USA

www.ankerpub.com

Library of Congress Cataloging-in-Publication Data
Service-learning code of ethics / Andrea Chapdelaine . . . [et al.].
    p. cm.
Includes bibliographical references and index.
  ISBN 1-882982-83-5
  1. Student service—Moral and ethical aspects—United States.
  I. Chapdelaine, Andrea.

LC220.5.S457 2005
378'.014—dc22
                                                    2005001833

About the Authors

Since we contributed equally to the development and writing of this book, the order of names is alphabetical.

Andrea Chapdelaine received her B.A. in psychology and justice studies from the University of New Hampshire and her Ph.D. in social psychology from the University of Connecticut. Now at Albright College, she is acting vice president of academic affairs and an associate professor in psychology. Previous articles on service-learning pedagogy have appeared in *Teaching of Psychology* and *CUR Quarterly*.

Ana Ruiz is an associate professor at Alvernia College. She earned a bachelor's degree at Catholic University of Pernambuco while growing up in Brazil. She completed her master's degree in cognitive development at Federal University of Pernambuco and obtained a doctoral degree in developmental psychology from Cornell University. She has used service-learning mostly in undergraduate research courses or outcome evaluations programs. In June 2003 she received a Campus Compact grant to identify the effect of service-learning experience on alumni employment choices and community engagement. She has also participated in several conferences discussing service-learning issues in general and the ethics of service-learning in particular.

Judith Warchal earned her B.A. in elementary/special education from King's College, her M.S. in rehabilitation counseling from the University of Scranton, and her Ph.D. in counseling psychology from Lehigh University. She is an associate professor of psychology and coordinator of the Master of Arts in Community

Counseling at Alvernia College. She is a licensed psychologist with a clinical practice at the Center for Mental Health at The Reading Hospital and Medical Center. Her research interests include service-learning, program evaluation, and mental health issues of the elderly.

 *Carole Wells* is an associate professor of psychology and interim assistant dean at Kutztown University. She developed an interest in psychology while an undergraduate at LaSalle University. She received her Ph.D. in social psychology and human resource management from Temple University. In addition to service-learning as pedagogy, her research focuses on trust, strategies of influence, and leadership in organizations; post-retirement activities of leaders and nonleaders; and conflict and conflict resolution.

Table of Contents

Foreword

In service-learning circles one frequently hears the claim that service-learning has now moved from the margins to the mainstream. Indeed, the very first chapter of *Service-Learning Code of Ethics* cites some of the data that helps to substantiate this claim. A more anecdotal verification of the same claim would be to note that it is increasingly difficult to stay abreast of the available service-learning literature.

And yet, as this book points out, there are still significant gaps in that literature, one of them being the lack of any systematic discussion of the ethical issues raised by service-learning practice and encountered by service-learning practitioners. The present volume seeks to address this gap. In both its assessment of the importance of exploring this topic and its own efforts to do so, this book puts all of us who are committed to the scholarship of engagement very much in its debt.

Service-Learning Code of Ethics contains at least three kinds of material that should be of interest to service-learning practitioners. First, it offers a general introduction to ethics as an essential dimension of service-learning planning and practice. Second, it identifies, articulates, and organizes specific ethical issue areas such as student, faculty, and administration responsibilities and questions related to liability. Third, it provides a model for how faculty can help make ethical considerations an essential part of the service-learning experience. In doing so, it further enriches the pedagogical value of service-learning by making available new reflection resources.

There are, however, still other, less direct ways in which this book assists the service-learning community. Of special importance is the way in which its faculty code of ethics clearly reinforces the difference between service-learning as an academy-community *partnership* and more traditional notions of student *placement* in the community. No faculty member reading and honoring the faculty code could fail to appreciate the importance of regular and substantive communication with his or her community partner(s). Indeed, all three codes—student, faculty, and administration—represent a kind of aspirational measure of our willingness to work toward truly respectful, reciprocal partnerships.

Service-Learning Code of Ethics reminds us at every turn of the importance of seeing civic and moral values as necessarily connected. This is the same point Colby, Ehrlich, Beaumont, and Stephens (2003) insist upon in their *Educating Citizens: Preparing America's Undergraduates for Lives of Civic and Moral Responsibility,* and the authors of the present text clearly acknowledge their indebtedness to that publication. This civic-moral connection is especially important, because of the clear need for supporters of civic renewal to find more effective ways to describe that renewal in the language of morality and personal values. By stressing the kinds of individual responsibility that inform service-learning practice, the authors help those inside and outside the academy to see more clearly the many ways service-learning can be linked to character development, leadership programs, honors programs, and codes of conduct. In doing so, they help "domesticate" social action within the pervasive American concern with personal behavior.

Campus Compact's "Pyramid of Service-Learning" postulates that as service-learning programs become more mature, they begin to take on the task of defining quality, making available or even requiring faculty training and consultation before a course can officially carry a "service-learning" designation. Until now, almost all of this work of certification has revolved around academic rigor, adequate reflection mechanisms, and community consultation. If the codes of ethics explored in the following pages were to be made a central part of the way in which more developed service-learning programs set the bar for exemplary practice, we could well see, in a few years' time, a richness of practice far beyond that of the present. It is my personal hope that, at the very least, this book will become as ubiquitous and well thumbed as a phone book in service-learning offices around the country.

Edward Zlotkowski
Senior Faculty Fellow, Campus Compact
Professor of English, Bentley College

Preface

Academicians increasingly argue that civic engagement is a moral imperative of institutions of higher learning. Educators are morally obligated to teach students the importance of civic responsibility, socially responsible behavior, and good citizenship skills. One effective pedagogical strategy used to meet these goals is service-learning—"meaningful community service that is linked to students' academic experience through related course materials and reflective activities" (Zlotkowski, 1998, p. 3). It is "education that impels students toward the formation of values" (Saltmarsh, 1997, p. 83).

Student engagement in service-learning is an ideal way to meet community needs, satisfy an institution's mission, and develop diversity awareness (Bringle & Hatcher, 2002; Dunlap, 2000; Eyler & Giles, 1999; O'Grady, 2000; Valerius & Hamilton, 2001). More importantly, service-learning allows students to confront and develop their own values. Certainly, through the many facets of service learning (e.g., preparatory training, community engagement, reflection), students encounter and wrestle with real ethical dilemmas.

Despite a tremendous amount of writing and research on the mechanics of doing service-learning (e.g., Bringle, Phillips, & Hudson, 2004; Dunlap, 1998; Ferrari & Jason, 1996; Howard, 1993; Kendall, 1991; Kretchmar, 2001; Markus, Howard, & King, 1993) and its benefits to learning (Bringle & Duffy, 1998; Campus Compact, 1993; Sax & Astin, 1997; Sigmon, 1994; Zlotkowski, 1996), there is a paucity of literature on the ethical challenges involved with this pedagogical undertaking, especially in higher education (Lisman, 1999; Schaffer, Paris, & Vogel, 2003).

Given the lack of available resources, institutions are ill prepared to respond to the inevitable ethical concerns that arise in service-learning. The purpose of this book is to fill the aforementioned void in the literature and begin to address these critical ethical issues in service-learning. We do not purport to resolve these issues, but by stimulating thinking and facilitating discussion, administrators, educators, students, and community agencies can be better prepared for the sometimes difficult ethical and moral dilemmas that arise during the service-learning process.

Audience

This book will benefit all those involved in service-learning—university administrators, instructors, and students. We wrote this primarily as a text for those college courses that incorporate service-learning into the curriculum. The practice of service-learning involves a multidisciplinary approach. Accordingly, this book will prepare instructors from a variety of disciplines for some of the ethical dilemmas likely to arise, and it will provide an ethical framework for student reflection and value development. Through reading, reflection, class discussion, and debate on the ethical issues presented, students will better understand these issues and be prepared to resolve the ethical dilemmas they encounter in their service-learning experiences. Administrators will be more aware of their ethical response and will be able to support faculty and students when challenged by ethical issues in service-learning.

Organization of the Book

This book is divided into five major sections. The first chapter in Part I presents an overview of service-learning and its role in American higher education. The second chapter is the cornerstone of the text. In this chapter we present 1) a synopsis of the theoretical context of moral decision-making; 2) a review of existing professional codes of ethics; 3) ethical principles that are most relevant to ethical decision-making in the service-learning context; 4) a proposed code of ethics (the Service-Learning Code of Ethics, or SLC), divided into three sections, one for each of the constituent groups (students, faculty, and administrators); and 5) a model of ethical decision-making.

The next three parts of the book address the SLC for students, faculty, and administrators. An explanation and discussion of the relevant section of the SLC is followed by a hypothetical dilemma. Following the dilemma, we apply the model for resolving ethical dilemmas. This is followed, when appropriate, by a section titled "Related Issues." Although not the central focus of the ethical dilemma, these issues are relevant and of sufficient importance to include. Related issues show the ethical dilemma in the larger service-learning context. Each hypothetical-dilemma chapter concludes with the presentation of a similar dilemma for class discussion and reflection and a set of questions to help guide the reader through the decision-making process. It is important to note that all dilemmas are hypothetical, although they speak to the universality of the dilemmas encountered in service-learning.

Although the hypothetical dilemmas are organized by constituency, all dilemmas involve issues germane to all groups. For example, dilemmas in the administrator section can be used to expand students' understanding of the broader issues involved in service-learning.

The last part of the book contains two concluding chapters. Much of the service-learning literature (Bringle, Phillips, & Hudson, 2004) is focused on assessment issues. Accordingly, Chapter 19 reviews current literature on formative and summative assessment in service-learning. It also includes a set of templates to assess the extent to which one has adhered to our proposed service-learning code. These forms measure specific items in the code, *not* how certain principles or values were met. Using the book as a facilitative guide, students, faculty, and administrators must examine their own values in light of their service-learning experiences.

Chapter 20 is an overview of risk management in service-learning. Although ethical and legal concerns in service-learning may be viewed as distinct, a significant amount of overlap does exist. To make that overlap more transparent, this chapter discusses valuable risk management steps that can be taken not only to help alleviate risk, but also to facilitate adherence to our proposed Service-Learning Code of Ethics. This chapter should only serve as a general guideline for risk management, since much is dependent on factors specific to a particular service-learning project (e.g., type of academic institution, geographical location and legal jurisdiction, and nature of project). Readers should consult with their institution's legal representatives for more specific information.

The appendix contains a diverse set of additional hypothetical dilemmas. Since these dilemmas are not related to any particular section of the code (i.e., type of constituent), several perspectives can be considered. The hypothetical dilemmas are followed by a set of questions to guide the reader through the model of ethical decision-making.

Service-Learning Code of Ethics is designed to provide a basic road map for navigating the complicated path of service-learning. It is a tool for reflection, exploration, judgment, and action, and we hope that this tool will be widely used, discussed, debated, and critiqued. It is only through such active engagement with complex ethical dilemmas that careful and deliberate decisions and optimal student learning are possible.

Acknowledgments

Although we take full responsibility for the ideas and content of this book, there are numerous individuals to thank for their support, guidance, and contributions. First, and foremost, are the many service-learning scholars and practitioners who have provided the groundwork for many of the ideas presented in this text. In particular, thank you to those colleagues and participants at various professional conferences held in 2004 (e.g., American Psychological Association, Eastern Psychological Association, International Service-Learning Research Conference, National Society for Experiential Education, and Society for the Psychological Study of Social Issues) who offered constructive criticism and feedback.

We thank our students, who provided insights into service-learning activities and helped shape the content of many of the hypothetical dilemmas. We also thank Robert Watrous, Kutztown University, whose expertise in student affairs and civic engagement helped in the development of our thinking about ethics in service-learning. Special thanks go to our institutions for providing various resources and accommodations to ensure that this book was completed in a timely fashion.

We sincerely appreciate the editorial support and valuable suggestions offered, at various stages in the development of this book, by Alysha Oswald. And we thank our publisher, James Anker, who saw the potential in this project, and Edward Zlotkowski and John Saltmarsh, who provided valuable advice and direction early in the process.

Finally, we owe special appreciation to our families. We could not have completed this book without their tireless support, devotion, and sacrifice.

PART I

Introduction

Chapter One

Overview of Service-Learning

One of the central purposes of higher education in the United States is to teach each new generation of citizens the democratic ideals of the nation, build moral character, and cultivate an educated, engaged citizenry (Lucas, 1994). Building upon that long-standing tradition, a significant number of colleges have revised their mission statements to embrace more fully these ideals, and they have taken significant steps to position themselves as responsible and responsive participants in the life of their surrounding communities (Chambers & Burkhardt, 2004). The Center for Liberal Education and Civic Engagement, established through a partnership between Campus Compact and the Association of American Colleges and Universities (AACU) to deepen understanding of the relation of liberal education to civic responsibilities, sets forth the following principles:

- A 21st Century liberal education must provide students with the knowledge and commitment to be socially responsible citizens in a diverse democracy and increasingly interconnected world.

- Colleges and Universities committed to liberal education have important civic responsibilities to their communities, their nation, and the larger world.

- Civic Engagement involves true partnerships, often between the institution and the community in which it is residing that serves mutual, yet independent interests, thereby honoring the integrity of all partners.

- Students' service activities can best serve society and the academy when connected directly to academic work, courses, and activities. (Campus Compact, 2004)

Moreover, approximately 500 college and university presidents have now signed the Declaration on the Civic Responsibility of Higher Education, which states:

> We challenge higher education to re-examine its public purposes and its commitments to the democratic ideal. We also challenge higher education to become engaged, through actions and teaching, with its communities. We have a fundamental task to renew our role as agents of our democracy. (Campus Compact, 1999)

Included in this commitment is a call not only for the university, but for the students themselves, to be civically engaged. "The civic mandate of liberal education is to develop in students the deepest knowledge base and the highest degree of critical independence possible to undergird informed, socially responsible judgments as voters, parents, consumers, professionals" (Stoddard & Cornwell, 2003, p. 44). The aforementioned presidential declaration further states:

> This country cannot afford to educate a generation that acquires knowledge without ever understanding how that knowledge can benefit society or how to influence democratic decision-making. We must teach the skills and values of democracy, creating innumerable opportunities for our students to practice and reap the results of the real, hard work of citizenship. (Campus Compact, 1999)

Yet, this growing call for a commitment to civic engagement in higher education has not gone unquestioned (Colby, Ehrlich, Beaumont, & Stephens, 2003; Ehrlich, 2000; Fish, 2003; Kenny, Simon, Brabeck, & Lerner, 2002; Mallory & Thomas, 2003; Schneider, 2004; Stamm, 2004). It has been debated whether colleges and universities should be teaching values, even those deemed essential to a democratic society (Barber, 2000; Callan, 1997; Galston, 1991; Young, 1997). We argue that there is merit in the teaching of values. Further, for many academic institutions, value acquisition is consistent with their mission statements.

Regardless of one's stance on the values issue, we believe that the primary focus should not be on whether students or other members of the college community come to adopt a certain set of values (a prescriptive approach), but instead on whether the college and its faculty provide and teach a process for exploring and critically reflecting upon the students' own value systems. Ehrlich (2003) states:

> Those of us who teach materials that particularly lend themselves to raising moral and civic issues have an obligation to do so in ways that help students wrestle with their own moral dilemmas as well as with larger social and political concerns. It is not enough simply to show that any moral framework built by reason can be criticized by reason, but rather we must also take on the much more difficult task of helping students to think through for themselves which moral perspective is best able to answer their intellectual, personal, and social needs. (pp. 3–4)

Service-learning does provide the opportunity for students to practice citizenship and engage in value exploration, and thus is viewed by many as an ideal way to achieve the vision set forth by this goal of a liberal education. "By aiming to provide students with an active, engaged environment for deepened learning and an awakened commitment to community and civic engagement, service-learning is amongst the most progressive pedagogies" (Oates & Leavitt, 2003, p. 7). It is a teaching tool that fosters the development of democratic principles such as tolerance, fairness, concern and respect for others, and a sense of responsibility to be civically knowledgeable and active. Such education is critical for the continuation of a self-governing society. "Service-learning contributes to returning higher education to its broader public mission: graduating students for responsible, active citizenship" (Oates & Leavitt, p. 5).

Given its strong association with the renewed commitment to civic engagement, the expansion of service learning during the past decade has been unprecedented. In the 2003 annual membership survey involving the participation of 402 campuses, Campus Compact found that 36% of students had participated in some form of service-learning (a record number since they conducted their first survey in 1987), 83% of the campuses had a community service or service-learning office to support such activity, and 25% reported that faculty involvement in service-learning has increased 10% or more in the past three years.

Similarly, according to a 2002 survey administered by The Policy Center on the First Year of College, approximately 60% of the institutions surveyed (1,000 colleges and universities participated) offer some type of service-learning experience in their first-year courses. Such growth is also reflected in the frequent mention of service-learning at national conferences of higher education (e.g., American Association for Higher Education, Association of American Colleges and Universities) and in their publications.

Along with the growth in service-learning, the obligation to address the role of value exploration and values clarification is becoming increasingly clear as students, faculty, and administrators wrestle with the practical complexities and ethical dilemmas that accompany the practice of service-learning. By its very nature service-learning supports Dewey's (1916/1997) well-entrenched maxim that optimal learning occurs through active engagement with the course material (Zlotkowski, 1998). Key elements include 1) the provision of a service by students to address a community need, 2) matching of the service activity to course learning objectives, and 3) reflective thinking. Bringle and Hatcher (1995) provide one of the most comprehensive and widely used definitions of service-learning, describing it as a

> course-based, credit-bearing educational experience that allows students to (a) participate in an organized service activity that meets identified community needs and (b) reflect on the service activity in such a way as to gain further understanding of course content, a broader appreciation of the discipline, and an enhanced sense of civic responsibility. (p. 112)

Consistent with these definitions, educational research has demonstrated that students gain more when they fully engage in and critically reflect upon the course material. These are elements that service-learning is uniquely designed to provide (Astin, 1991; Eyler & Giles, 1999; Jacoby, 1996; Kaye, 2003; Nist & Holschuh, 1999; Pascarella & Terenzini, 1991). Research on service-learning has also shown an impact on other kinds of learning, including increases in theoretical understanding, cognitive complexity, and ability to apply knowledge to novel problems (Astin & Sax, 1998; Markus, Howard, & King, 1993; Osborne, Hammerich, & Hensley, 1998; Strage, 2000; Vogelgesang & Astin, 2000).

Thus service-learning, based in experiential learning, affords a unique and valuable opportunity for student value exploration and development. Students participating in community-service experiences encounter ethical dilemmas that challenge their own value systems and the ideals of an American democracy. By grappling with such dilemmas, formulating and acting upon a method of resolution, and then reflecting upon the consequences of a chosen course of action, students achieve the value clarification and civic engagement goals of a liberal education. Through active involvement in this process, the same end may be achieved for faculty and administrators. In this way, American institutions of higher education play a role in cultivating citizens committed to the public good and of benefit to their communities.

Again, research has supported these hypotheses. Service-learning does increase commitment to civic responsibility (Astin & Sax, 1998; Giles & Eyler, 1994; Kendrick, 1996; Myers-Lipton, 1996), tolerance toward and understanding of diverse others (Bringle & Kremer, 1993; Eyler, Giles, & Braxton, 1997; Juhn et al., 1999; Osborne et al., 1998), prosocial behaviors (Batchelder & Root, 1994; Markus et al., 1993), and moral development (Boss, 1994; Gorman, Duffy, & Heffernan, 1994). However, the question of how all of this happens remains unanswered, as stated below:

> While many colleges and universities make explicit statements about the goal of civic engagement, few have fully incorporated the development of a student's civic character into curricular programs, despite the research that demonstrates the benefits of linking theory and practice to an individual's intellectual growth. Additionally, an overwhelming number of colleges and universities have within their mission statements reference to civic responsibility, without describing how this happens. (Oates & Leavitt, 2003, p. 5)

In order for students to achieve the goal of greater civic engagement through service-learning experiences, best practices of service-learning (Honnet & Poulson, 1989) suggest the following is required: 1) adequate preparation for service-learning experiences; 2) demonstration of how such experiences relate to the learning objectives (e.g., tools to engage in value development); 3) an active and instrumental role in the service-learning project; and, most important, 4) an opportunity to reflect upon these experiences and place them in the context of the learning objectives and the larger mission of civic engagement.

Leming (2001) found that high school students who had ethical decision-making material integrated with their service-learning were significantly more systematic in their ethical reasoning and more likely to use an ethical viewpoint than those who participated in service-learning without this curriculum. Similar results with college students were found by Gorman, Duffy, and Heffernan (1994).

However, without clear guidelines about ethical decision-making practices, the process seems haphazard at best.

Summary

Higher education currently professes a significant commitment to a mission of civic engagement. Academe as a whole has embraced many avenues by which to connect to and benefit its surrounding community and beyond. Service-learning is ideal for this commitment to the community because it relies heavily on the proven pedagogical method of active learning. Yet it often has been assumed that by simply partaking in service-learning experiences, civic engagement will be an inevitable result for the institution, faculty, and students.

We call for the recognition and examination of the ethical challenges one faces in service-learning experiences. In order for such ethical challenges to affect service-learning practitioners in a way that fosters democratic ideals, a set of pedagogical tools is required. These tools include guidelines, or what is more commonly called a *code of ethics,* specific to the service-learning context. Individuals must carefully examine this code (through reading, discussion, and written and oral analysis), practice it through hypothetical applications, actively use the code when faced with actual service-learning dilemmas, and finally, reflect critically upon these experiences. That set of tools is what comprises the body of this book. We recognize that developing a code of ethics is only one of many steps that must be taken to better connect service-learning to the goals of higher education, but we believe it is a critical element without which other efforts may not be as productive.

Chapter Two

Service-Learning Code of Ethics

Morality, Values, and Ethics

The terms *morals, values,* and *ethics* are often used interchangeably to refer to the practices that enable a society to operate in the best interest of all its citizens. In the United States, those practices are articulated as the democratic ideals first promoted by the founding fathers and expanded through the democratic process. Ehrlich (2000) states, "America's democratic principles, including tolerance and respect for others, procedural impartiality, and concern for both the rights of the individual and the welfare of the group, are all grounded in moral principles" (p. 1). Morals are ideas about what is right and wrong. Morality is about the relationships between people and how they agree to live in a manner that protects the best interests of all. Morality also involves language and vocabulary "that permit the members of the society to engage in moral discourse for the purpose of evaluating the actions of individuals and the practices and institutions of the society" (Boatright, 2000, p. 23). Morality is not necessarily tied to religion, but is about the values a society holds dear. A moral dilemma occurs when there is a conflict between values and ideas about what is moral.

Values are the specific qualities that together comprise the morality of a society. Usually values involve the qualities that provide direction in everyday life. Some of these values may be culture-specific, while others are universal.

> Values represent the comparative worth ascribed to things, whether of a tangible or intangible nature. A value orientation serves, in part, to shape the nature of

the ethical principles themselves, which then can be used as more explicit guidelines against which to measure individual behavior.... What is judged to be ethical in making these kinds of choices is a manifestation of values about what outcomes are more important than others, and about what actions and risks are reasonable and acceptable in seeking to reach these objectives. (Snow, Grady, & Goyette-Ewing, 2000, pp. 899–900)

Thus, values are essential to ethical decision-making, in that they direct the process.

Ethics are often considered to be the results of systematic reflection on morality and values (Purtilo, 1999). The study of ethics involves a process of deciding the best course of action when faced with a given situation. There are many ethical theories that can serve as guides in the decision-making process. Understanding the complexities of the theories can be a challenging endeavor that requires a strong background in philosophy. A complete review of these theories is beyond the scope of this book, but a broad outline follows; the reader is encouraged to explore further the philosophical foundations of ethical thought.

In what is probably an oversimplification, ethical theories can be divided into one of three categories: rule ethics, virtue ethics, and feminist ethics (Volbrecht, 2002). Rule ethics are concerned with answering the question, "What actions are right?" Rule ethics are derived from two classic ethics theories: deontological theories and teleological theories. Deontological theory, attributed to Immanuel Kant (1788/1949) and often referred to as Kantian theory, is based on an understanding of ethical action as resulting from duties and rights. It is every individual's moral obligation, according to this theory, to do what "ought" to be done. What ought to be done is determined by what every rational being would agree is right. In general, it is akin to a universal law (rule) based on respect for human dignity. In this theory, every individual carries an inherent dignity and is therefore entitled to respect. Kant believed that some actions are inherently immoral, regardless of their consequences, and thus the means of the decision, not just the ends, must be considered. This theory may be problematic when duties or rights conflict.

Teleological theory (also referred to as utilitarianism), another rule-based theory, is concerned with the consequences of one's actions. Decisions are made based on the greatest balance of good over evil, or the greater good. Teleological theories are most closely associated with the work of Jeremy Bentham (1789/1939) and John Stuart Mill (1859/1939). The focus is on the action and the consequence. One should choose the action that will provide the greatest good to the greatest number of people. In essence, the end justifies the means. A difficulty with this theory is that to fully consider the consequences of one's actions, it would be necessary to have knowledge of all possible consequences related to the act, which is rarely possible.

The second broad category of ethical theory is virtue ethics. Virtue ethics are not concerned with the rule, duty, obligation, or consequence of right action, but rather with the moral character of the individual making the decision. Virtue ethics have their foundation in the work of Aristotle, who proposed that the good life could only be achieved by a virtuous person. Community life is an essential element of the theory, for the virtuous individual lives in a community of close interpersonal relationships.

The third broad category of ethical theory is the most recent. Feminist theory, often referred to as the ethics of care (Gilligan, 1982), has a broad focus on the institutional reduction of oppressive societal forces, specifically with regard to policies that affect historically oppressed groups such as women and minorities. Key to this theory is the issue of power and how power is used to oppress and devalue women. Proponents of feminist ethics argue that traditional approaches to ethics (e.g., Kant, Bentham, Mill, and Aristotle) were based on typically masculine ideals and virtues that diminished the value of relationships and caring. Noddings (1984), in developing a feminine, relational approach to ethics, suggests that real care involves actual encounters with people, not just good intentions.

Individually, none of these ethical theories presents a perfect framework for ethical behavior. For example, rule ethics appear to provide the conceptual tools for a precise, objective way of rationalizing ethical decisions; but individuals make ethical decisions with their hearts, not only with their minds. Virtuous people who have good moral character make decisions that do not always follow the rules, but these decisions are ethically defensible just the same. Critics of feminist ethics argue that the ethics of care is not a new ethical theory, since many of its characteristics are encompassed in the basic principle of benevolence. They argue that ethical theory is not and should not be gender specific. Even feminist ethicists agree that there is no single feminist perspective on any one moral issue. Thus the search for moral justifications through the application of ethical theories is far more complicated than it might first appear. Each encounter must be viewed as unique and examined in light of moral principles and all the constituencies involved. While community is an important concept in ethical decision-making, the resolution of an ethical dilemma requires a decision that balances the needs of the individual and society.

An ethical issue is any situation "embedded with important moral challenges" (Purtilo, 1999, p. 13). Ethical dilemmas have been defined as "situations when what is ethically correct is not clear, and any of several ethically defensible solutions may be arrived at, depending on one's analysis of the situation" (Weithorn, 1987, p. 230). Schaffer, Paris, and Vogel (2003) define an ethical problem in service-learning as "the experience of a conflict about the right thing to do" (p. 153). The dilemmas usually involve a conflict between two or more virtues (or principles) and two or more morally defensible courses of action. In other words, choosing one course of action (and following one virtue or principle) necessitates violating the other. In many cases, the ethical decision involves a judgment about which choice is the lesser of two evils (or the greater of two equal goods). Analysis is perhaps the most critical component of ethics. Through the analysis of the situation, the moral issues are defined, the value discrepancies identified, the conflicting principles acknowledged, and the potential solutions debated.

Ethical Deliberations in Service-Learning

Service-learning presents situations where one's analysis of the situation may depend heavily on the perspective being taken or the constituency being served. By definition, service-learning requires attention and responsibility to multiple constituencies, including students, faculty, the academic institution, and the community. The analysis must consider the interests of all parties. Thus the levels of analysis (e.g., a stated institutional policy on sexual harassment is the institutional level, whereas protecting a student from sexual harassment in the community is both an individual and institutional issue) are an important consideration when choosing an ethical course of action. Service-learning, by definition, requires careful and deliberate reflection on the service project and an integration of the service with the academic goals. The reflection requirement provides an excellent opportunity for deliberation over and analysis of the ethical issues encountered in service-learning.

Professional Codes of Ethics

Codes of conduct have been widely established by many professional organizations to provide guidelines for professional behavior and for analysis of ethically difficult situations. These codes serve the dual purpose of protecting the community being served by the profession and providing the professionals with a framework of best practices. Ethical codes are usually the result of the need for a moral lens through which professionals can evaluate the practical dilemmas encountered in a particular profession. Professional codes of conduct seek to provide both mandatory and aspirational goals for the profession. However, no code of ethics can guarantee ethical behavior or resolve all of the ethical dilemmas faced by members of the profession. Codes of ethics have many limitations and are generally self-imposed by members of a profession. There is rarely complete agreement by members of the profession as to what constitutes right and wrong behavior; but, despite the inherent difficulties, Corey, Corey, and Callahan (1998) suggest that "Ethical codes are necessary, but not sufficient, for exercising ethical responsibility" (p. 7). Ethically responsible practice in any profession requires a careful examination of the individual and cultural circumstances of the situation.

Service-learning is no different. While not a profession itself, service-learning presents unique issues, problems, and situations for those who engage in it. In writing about the moral obligations of professors, Tellez (2000) sounds a caution that "no attention was given to the moral dilemmas faced by professors who require service learning" (p. 77). Tellez suggests that three of the nine principles for moral decision-making by college professors developed by Murray, Gillese, Lennon, Mercer, and Robinson (1996) directly apply to service-learning. These principles are 1) a necessity for pedagogical competence, 2) the need to deal with sensitive topics, and 3) the focus on student development. As more college professors require service-learning, the ethical dilemmas become more apparent.

Thus, our search for ethical guidelines for service-learning began with discipline-specific codes of ethics. It is easy to find a code of ethics for psychologists, physical therapists, health care professionals, chemists, engineers, accountants, social workers, and music educators (American Association of University Professors [AAUP], 1990; American Counseling Association, 1995; American Medical Association, 2001; American Society of Civil Engineers, 1996; National Association of Social Workers, 1999; National Organization for Human Service Education, 1996; National Society of Professional Engineers, 2003). Educators, as professionals in their chosen fields, also are often bound by the code of ethics specific to their fields. However, these codes do not address ethical issues relevant to the service-learning experience, although the majority of these codes include a mandate to provide a benefit to the community.

For example, the AAUP is widely recognized as the premier organization for facilitating the practice of teaching in colleges and universities. Interestingly, John Dewey, who is often considered the guiding force behind the current service-learning movement, served as the first chair of the AAUP's committee on university ethics in 1916. Although it does not address issues specifically related to service-learning, AAUP's (1990) Statement on Professional Ethics does instruct professors to "demonstrate respect for students as individuals and adhere to their proper roles as intellectual guides and counselors" (p. 76). Similarly, the American Council on Education (1995–2005) developed a set of strategic priorities, one of which focuses on service designed to "support colleges, universities, and other higher education and adult learning organizations in their efforts to serve students and society."

A review of the codes of ethics for specific professions reveals some noteworthy mandates that can be viewed as a justification for a service-learning curriculum. Professionals, who are charged with training the next generation of experts in their fields, demonstrate by example the elements of the code. Many codes include specific references to civic responsibility and leadership. For example, Section 10-d of the American Counseling Association's (1995) Code of Ethics discusses pro bono service. It states, "Counselors contribute to society by devoting a portion of their professional activity to services for which there is little or no financial return."

Similarly, the Ethical Standards of Human Service Professionals states,

> Human service professionals, regardless of whether they
> are students, faculty or practitioners, promote and
> encourage the unique values and characteristics of

human service. In so doing human service professionals uphold the integrity and ethics of the profession, partake in constructive criticism of the profession, promote the client and community well-being, and enhance their professional growth. (National Organization for Human Service Education, 1996)

In addition, the National Association of Social Workers (1999) Code of Ethics states, "Social workers promote social justice and social change with and on behalf of clients." It also mandates, "The Code socializes practitioners new to the field to social work's mission, values, ethical principles, and ethical standards."

In another example, Section III-2a of the Code of Engineers (National Society of Professional Engineers, 2003) states, "Engineers shall seek opportunities to be of constructive service in civic affairs and work for the advancement of the safety, health and well-being of their community." And, Section 7 of the Principles of Medical Ethics of the American Medical Association (2001) states, "A physician shall recognize a responsibility to participate in activities contributing to an improved society."

For examples of other ethical codes of conduct, with specific reference to social responsibility in the training of new professionals, the reader is encouraged to review Section IV of the Code of Ethical Conduct of the National Association for the Education of Young Children (1998), Professional Obligations of the American Society of Civil Engineers' (1996) Code of Ethics, Section 3.1 of the Association for Computing Machinery (1997), the American Society for Public Administration (2000) Code of Ethics, and the Chartered Financial Analyst (1999; formerly Association for Investment Management and Research) Code of Ethics.

These codes mandate civic engagement in general, but much like current discourses on service-learning, they don't specifically discuss how to engage in service-learning in an ethical way. At its core, service-learning is about relationships among faculty, students, the college or university, and community agencies, each group having different agendas, resources, and levels of power. A code of conduct is needed to provide standards and guidelines for appropriate professional conduct, roles, and responsibilities to guide the interaction among those involved in service-learning as well as the products of their labors. However, as indicated, no single existing code of ethics applies specifically to service-learning. Therefore, we propose a set of principles as guidelines for ethical decision-making in service-learning experiences. Based on these principles, we propose a code specifically for service-learning and a model by which these principles can be applied to resolve an ethical dilemma encountered in service-learning. The principles proposed are beneficence, nonmaleficence, justice/fairness/equity, fidelity/responsibility, autonomy and respect for people's rights, and integrity.

Ethical Principles

Beneficence is the act of doing good. The focus is on the promotion of good in service to others. The question of doing good leads to the question of "Good in whose best interest?" This principle is dependent on how one defines good and goodness.

Nonmaleficence means doing no harm, doing no evil, protecting others from harm. This involves acts of commission as well as omission. It involves knowing the limitations of one's expertise when serving others, and recognizing that even the best actions may have some harmful effects.

Justice/fairness/equity refer to impartiality, fair representation of facts, consistency, and comparable treatment of diverse populations and groups. Service involves The Golden Rule: Do unto others as you would have them do unto you.

Fidelity/responsibility have to do with trustworthiness, faithfulness, performance, and careful observation of service obligations.

Autonomy and respect for people's rights refer to the promotion of self-determination—the freedom of the individual to choose his or her own destiny. Students, institutions, community agencies, and community participants should have an active role in service.

Integrity refers to accuracy and truthfulness in the practice of service. It involves the idea that honesty is important when dealing with others. Deception should be avoided.

Service-Learning Code of Ethics

Ethical concerns and dilemmas in service-learning involve multiple constituents. Based on the aforementioned ethical principles, we propose a code of ethics for service-learning involving students, faculty, and administrators.

The code does not include guidelines for community agency personnel, because they will be guided by agency policies and the code of ethics of their professional disciplines.

I. Students

1) Students in service-learning shall behave as professional representatives of the college/university at all times.

2) Students in service-learning shall understand their role and its limitations in the context of the service-learning assignment.

3) Students in service-learning shall adhere to the policies and procedures of the community agency.

4) Students in service-learning shall treat service recipients in a manner consistent with ethical principles.

5) Students in service-learning shall fulfill their service-learning commitment to the agency in accordance with the course requirements.

6) Students in service-learning shall agree to abide by any applicable legal and ethical guidelines.

7) Students in service-learning shall recognize and reflect upon potential challenges to their personal value systems.

8) Students in service-learning shall carefully consider all aspects of the service-learning assignment and consult with faculty members if participation would cause undue distress due to personal circumstances.

II. Faculty

1) Faculty shall match community needs with academic service-learning goals prior to the beginning of the project to ensure that academic and community service goals can be achieved.

2) Faculty shall minimize potential harm to agencies, their constituents, and students.

3) Faculty shall provide community agencies with a plan that includes information about what is expected and required of students and the agency (e.g., accountability, commitment, consistency, and communication).

4) Faculty shall develop course goals consistent with service-learning objectives and communicate to the students, both verbally and in writing, the parameters of the service-learning requirement, including:

   a) Academic objectives for the service-learning experience

   b) Articulated community benefits

   c) Time requirements

   d) Students' roles and responsibilities

   e) Legal and ethical guidelines on issues such as professionalism, liability, confidentiality, and insurance

   f) Responses to emergencies (e.g., threats, weather, and health risks)

   g) Expectations for integration into course material and reflection

   h) Alternative assignment unless college policy requires service-learning

5) Faculty shall properly train and inform students of their responsibilities and potential risks prior to the beginning of the service-learning activity.

6) Faculty shall ensure that students understand the diverse characteristics of those with whom they will be working.

7) Faculty shall treat all students in a manner consistent with ethical principles.

8) Faculty shall maintain involvement with community agencies throughout the process and be responsive to changing needs and circumstances.

9) Faculty shall be available to students for consultation or referral for problem solving and conflict resolution.

10) Faculty shall assess the outcomes of this activity for the recipients, the community, and students.

III. Administrators

1) Administrators shall recognize and support opportunities for service-learning as part of a liberal education.

2) Administrators shall provide mechanisms for the institutionalization of civic engagement and resources for service-learning participation and service-related research.

3) Administrators shall be sensitive to and knowledgeable about community needs.

4) Administrators shall make every effort to minimize risky and unsafe locations and circumstances.

5) Administrators shall provide clear guidelines to faculty and students regarding liability and ethical issues.

6) Administrators shall provide faculty with opportunities for training and education in service-learning curriculum infusion.

7) Administrators shall treat all constituents in a manner consistent with ethical principles.

Model of Ethical Decision-Making

Most models of decision-making follow similar steps with some minor variations (Corey, Corey, & Haynes, 1998; Kearsley, 2003; Purtilo, 1999). Using the above ethical principles and code of ethics, we propose the following six-step model of ethical decision-making applied to service-learning (see Table 2.1).

TABLE 2.1

Model of Ethical Decision-Making

Step 1:	Identify and define the dilemma.
Step 2:	Address relevant principles and gather information.
Step 3:	Propose courses of action.
Step 4:	Determine and analyze the consequences for each proposed course of action.
Step 5:	Decide on the best course of action.
Step 6:	Evaluate and reflect on the decision.

The first step is to identify and define the dilemma. In this step, one must clearly delineate the dilemma so that all options can be analyzed. It is easier to solve a specific problem than a vague one; therefore, simplifying the problem and highlighting the most important factors are critical. Often there are competing goals to which different ethical principles could apply. In addition, the same ethical principle could mean different courses of action to different parties.

The second step is to address relevant principles and gather information. Sources include the principles, laws and regulations, and codes that may be applicable, and consultation with experts (e.g., supervisors, instructors, coworkers, and administrators). The person can then analyze the available information, determine if more information is needed, and organize the information to develop possible resolutions.

The third step is to propose as many courses of action as possible. These should include factors relevant to effective decision-making. Several good alternatives and as many factors as possible should be generated. If there is a long list of actions, they should be grouped into related factors.

The fourth step is to determine and analyze the consequences for each proposed course of action. These courses of action should be examined cautiously and defensively. That is, one should attempt to see why each proposed action might not work, as a way to highlight weak points. Based on this analysis, one can then eliminate or alter actions, or prepare contingency plans to counter possible negative outcomes.

The fifth step is to decide on the best course of action. If necessary, one should consult with appropriate sources to seek feedback on one's decision.

The final step is to evaluate and reflect on whether the selected course of action is the best one. This last step is crucial to moral growth through the resolution of the ethical dilemma. Among the many tests available, the pillow, newspaper, and child tests can be used to evaluate the decision selected. In these tests, the following questions can be posed and answered: Can you sleep with your decision? Would you be comfortable having your decision published in the newspaper? Would you tell a child to engage in this behavior?

PART II

Students

Chapter Three

Service-Learning
Code of Ethics for Students

S tudents are the primary participants in any service-learning experience. Without the student, there would be no reason for service-learning. Yet students are often unprepared for the practical and professional aspects of service-learning. Because most of them have work experience and understand the rules of the work world, faculty often assume that the "New Millennials" (students born after 1982) are more experienced and savvy than they prove to be. Growing up in a desegregated country does not mean that they have abandoned the prejudices that continue to haunt their parents' generation. Yet service-learning experiences often place students in situations that are quite different from their typical work or school experience, and they often find themselves floundering in a sea of expectations without clear direction. Many professional programs in colleges and universities provide students with instruction in ethics specific to their chosen discipline, but that training usually occurs in the final few courses of the student's senior year, during which practical experience may be required. Thus, students in the freshman through junior years of college may be involved in service-learning projects without any formal training in ethical practice. The student section of the Service-Learning Code of Ethics (SLC) was developed with this in mind.

The student section of the code is designed to provide students with specific guidelines for behavior and decision-making during service-learning experiences. Students will undoubtedly find themselves in situations that they are ill equipped to handle due to inexperience. The nature of many service-learning experiences places students in circumstances where they act alone or in small groups, often without direct supervision from faculty. The SLC for students is not intended to be all-inclusive, nor will it provide solutions to every problem students may encounter; it is instead designed to give students a benchmark for making good ethical choices.

The student section of the SLC makes explicit what faculty members might otherwise take for granted. It begins with a mandate that students behave as professional representatives of the college/university at all times. The first part of the student code depends heavily on faculty to explain to students what "professional" means for their particular institution and for the specific service-learning experience. Faculty preparation is a key component. Students cannot be expected to adhere to professional behavior if they have not received specific instruction in what "professional" looks like in the workplace. Equally important is the fact that the students are representing the academic institution in the community. One negative experience with a student has the potential of erasing years of positive interactions with a community partner. Students need to understand that their experience in the community affects more than just their own evaluations.

Students also need to understand that there are serious limitations to what they can and cannot do. Many times this takes the form of setting and maintaining appropriate boundaries for the activity. Students must recognize that when they agree to participate in a service-learning activity, they also agree to abide by the policies and procedures of the agency with which they are working. Again, this implies that the faculty member has ensured that the student will receive training in the appropriate policies and procedures of the agency, and that the agency agrees to provide the proper training.

The code for students stresses that all service recipients are treated with respect, honesty, fairness, and confidentiality. Higher education has a responsibility to promote the fundamental democratic principles of tolerance and respect for the diversity of human experience. Service-learning affords students the opportunity to recognize that they are members of a larger, diverse social context. Respect, honesty, and fairness are essential ingredients of any community-university partnership, and within a code of ethics, they provide a foundation for discourse about public issues.

When students agree to a service-learning project, they must fulfill their obligations to the community. If a student leaves the agency prior to completing the assignment, faculty and community staff are faced with either providing the service or abandoning the project. Presenting students with a specific code should help to underscore the seriousness of the experience and the potential legal implications involved.

The student code emphasizes that students may experience mild to intense personal reactions to the service-learning experience. Students may find their value systems challenged and perhaps changed through service-learning. Students need to know that there are resources available to them through faculty, community staff, or the college counseling center should they need assistance in coping with difficult situations and personal value exploration. The reflection central to the service-learning experience is an excellent opportunity for this process of inquiry. However, the code also recognizes that certain service-learning assignments may create a personal dilemma for a student who is unable to participate in the activity because of mitigating private circumstances. It is then the student's responsibility to consult with the faculty member to resolve the impasse in a way that does not compromise the integrity of the course assignments.

Ehrlich (2003), a proponent of service-learning as a tool for the development of moral and civic responsibility, states, "Higher education should encourage and facilitate the development of students' capacities to examine complex situations in which competing values are often at stake, to employ both substantive knowledge and moral reasoning to evaluate the problems and values involved, to develop their own judgments about those issues, and then to act on their judgments" (p. 2). A possible benefit of providing students with a code of ethics for service-learning is the opportunity to begin a dialogue that encourages ethical behavior in every setting, regardless of discipline. A just society depends on informed, committed, socially responsible leaders who practice ethical decision-making in every situation. Thus, the following student SLC is proposed.

I. Students

1) Students in service-learning shall behave as professional representatives of the college/university at all times.

2) Students in service-learning shall understand their role and its limitations in the context of the service-learning assignment.

3) Students in service-learning shall adhere to the policies and procedures of the community agency.

4) Students in service-learning shall treat service recipients in a manner consistent with ethical principles.

5) Students in service-learning shall fulfill their service-learning commitment to the agency in accordance with the course requirements.

6) Students in service-learning shall agree to abide by any applicable legal and ethical guidelines.

7) Students in service-learning shall recognize and reflect upon potential challenges to their personal value systems.

8) Students in service-learning shall carefully consider all aspects of the service-learning assignment and consult with faculty members if participation would cause undue distress due to personal circumstances.

Chapter Four

Conflict Between Student Personal Commitments and Service-Learning Requirement

Barry is a fourth-year social work major with a minor in Spanish. After graduation, he plans to work in the inner city in foster and adoptive family services, abuse assessment, and child advocacy. Barry believes that completing his Spanish minor will be a valuable tool in becoming a more effective social worker. At this point, he has completed 12 of the 18 credits required for the minor. Barry enrolls in a six-credit capstone class in advanced Spanish (i.e., Intensive Spanish III/IV). One of the graded requirements for this class is a 45-hour service-learning experience. Students in this class are to engage in various activities at a nonprofit agency for Hispanic immigrants, whose mission is to help its clients develop valuable life skills, educational enrichment, citizenship and leadership behavior, and resourcefulness.

The instructor, Dr. Jones, requires that students use their Spanish-speaking skills to tutor and mentor the children, adolescents, and adults served by this agency. Students will be helping clients with adjustment problems, homework, and assimilation into the community. Dr. Jones's goals for service-learners in the class are to improve their Spanish oral and written communication skills and enhance their understanding of Hispanic culture. She also expects students to speak Spanish in class while discussing their field experiences, including a reflection on their personal reactions to the tutoring experience and how cultural differences affect their work.

Most students in the class are able to balance this service-learning requirement with their other academic and work-related commitments. However, because Barry is married with a small child and has a full-time job as an assistant manager for a local convenience store, this assignment presents problems for him. Up to this point, his manager has been flexible and allowed him to take classes during the day and make up the hours in the evenings and on weekends.

Barry stays after the first class and explains to Dr. Jones that he cannot complete the service requirement, although he believes it would be beneficial to him. Dr. Jones reminds Barry that the syllabus clearly states this is a requirement for the class. She reviews past successes and tells Barry that she has been using this method of teaching conversational Spanish for the last five years. She assures him that any personal sacrifice he would need to make to complete this assignment would be well worth the effort.

Step 1: Identify and Define the Dilemma

The service-learning code provides a framework for understanding conflicting and competing personal and professional goals. Despite Barry's intentions to learn as much as possible in his classes and do well, he is experiencing conflict about completing the course. According to the code, students are required to *fulfill their service-learning commitment to the agency in accordance with the course requirements* (SLC I.5), and yet, *faculty must treat all students in a manner consistent with ethical principles* (SLC II.7).

According to Dr. Jones, her past practices in this course are clear to all students and her syllabus unambiguously outlines these requirements (SLC II.4). During her conversation with Barry, she points out that previous student experiences and the literature support this assignment as an extremely effective pedagogical strategy and a useful way to become skilled in conversational Spanish. She stresses the added benefit of enhanced class and group discussions. Dr. Jones, therefore, believes that in order to be fair to the other students in the class and provide a rich experience for Barry, he should be required to participate.

Step 2: Address Relevant Principles and Gather Information

As a nontraditional student, Barry always tries to see the bigger picture and appreciates his professors' efforts to apply course material to the "real world." He understands that Dr. Jones's interest in associating community service with academic experience is a profitable and useful way of skill development in Spanish. However, he feels that his personal, professional, and academic responsibilities are at odds with each other.

In this instance, as outlined and described in Chapter 2, the principle of beneficence, the act of doing good, suggests a mutually satisfying relationship between Barry and community agency clients. He will improve his ability to communicate with future clients and enhance his understanding of their culture. But, if he is promoting the good of agency clients, what about the good of his family and his responsibilities to them? Barry wrestles with the conflict between his personal responsibility to his wife and child and his academic responsibility. In other words, he is unsure how to resolve this dilemma in a fair and just way.

In an effort to gather more information and ideas, Barry talks to students who belong to a nontraditional student organization on campus. They recommend that he try to negotiate with the instructor a similar assignment or extra-credit work that would require less-structured, off-campus hours. His peers empathize with Barry and support his desire to do well and be as prepared as possible for future employment. They are concerned that this assignment might create an added burden that could adversely affect him physically, psychologically, and emotionally.

Step 3: Propose Courses of Action

Barry considers several options. He could:

- *Action A:* Drop his minor in Spanish and take two others courses to make up the six credits.

- *Action B:* Talk to Dr. Jones about offering an alternate assignment.

- *Action C:* Drop the class and delay graduation, hoping to reduce his work hours and take this course next semester.

- *Action D:* Request that his work hours be structured around the service-learning requirement, recognizing that this will be a difficult semester.

- *Action E:* Reduce his work hours and seek financial support.

Step 4: Determine and Analyze the Consequences for Each Proposed Course of Action

Action A: Drop his minor in Spanish and take two others courses to make up the six credits.

Positive. For Barry, dropping his minor in Spanish is a relatively straightforward and easy solution to this dilemma. He could drop this course and pick up six credits in two less-demanding free elective courses.

Negative. Because Barry is sure he ultimately wants to work closely with the Hispanic community, he thinks it would be a mistake to drop his minor in Spanish. He knows that some fluency in Spanish would add to his credibility and be useful with this population. Because the period for adding classes has passed, Barry would be able to drop this course but would have difficulty scheduling and obtaining permission from two professors to be added to their class rosters. In addition, he would lose his full-time status and financial aid if he cannot replace these six credits.

Action B: Talk to Dr. Jones about offering an alternate assignment.

Positive. Selecting an alternative to the service-learning requirement for this class would give Barry an opportunity to fulfill the course requirements, continue his current work schedule, satisfy his Spanish minor, and complete his degree requirements on time.

Negative. Barry is willing to consider other activities but recognizes that Dr. Jones offered no alternate options. At the same time, he realizes that the syllabus clearly outlines what is needed to earn the six credits in this class. As a conscientious and committed student, Barry has never asked for an exception to course requirements. He is unsure how this would affect faculty perceptions about his ability to be a flexible yet hard-working social worker.

Action C: Drop the class and delay graduation, hoping to reduce his work hours and take this course next semester.

Positive. This remains a viable option for Barry. He hopes that if he has an additional semester, he can develop a creative solution to meet both his workplace and home demands. This solution would reduce Barry's stress level and give him an opportunity to spend more time with his wife and child. In addition, he would not be rushing through the course and would be able to spend more time learning the material.

Negative. This solution would postpone Barry's ability to complete his degree in a timely fashion, obtain employment, and begin repaying his large debt. Barry believes achieving goals are part of being a good student, worker, and citizen. He regrets not being a serious and committed student when he was younger and is uncomfortable about deviating from his plans.

Action D: Request that his work hours be structured around the service-learning requirement, recognizing that this will be a difficult semester.

Positive. Barry is torn between discussing these demands on his schedule with his supervisor and finding other employment. He realizes that his boss has always been supportive and flexible in the past and is hopeful that his boss is once again willing to meet his needs.

Negative. Barry is concerned that if he asks his boss for one more scheduling change, he will be fired and then will have to search for other employment. This would be time-consuming and would create a financial hardship for his family. On the other hand, if Barry decides to continue in the class, he realizes this would be a difficult semester. He might be unable to contribute fully because of fatigue, stress, and time pressures. This could result in poor grades, reducing his chances of admission to a Masters of Social Work program later on. In addition, his health could suffer along with his marriage, creating a dilemma in his personal life not unlike the problems he hopes to help others resolve someday as a social worker.

Action E: Reduce his work hours and seek financial support.

Positive. Barry could reduce his weekly work hours and ask his wife to add more hours to her schedule at a fast-food restaurant. This option would afford him more time to study and also to work with clients and develop a better understanding of the Hispanic community and culture.

Negative. This does not seem to be a viable solution because Barry and his wife are already concerned about their current debt and the effect their work schedules will have on their two-year-old daughter. In addition, Barry has had a long-standing arrangement with his boss to work a fixed number of hours each week. If his boss is not amenable to reduced hours, Barry could lose his job. Because Barry and his wife have overextended themselves, resulting in poor credit, it is unlikely they would be able to borrow more money.

Step 5: Decide on the Best Course of Action

While none of the proposed courses of action provides an ideal solution for Barry, he decides on Action D, which is to request a change in his work hours. He explains the course requirement to his wife and boss and anticipates a stressful and demanding semester. Although his wife is not happy, she decides to be as supportive as possible. Reluctantly, Barry's boss is willing to make some minor adjustments, enabling Barry to change his work schedule slightly to accommodate the service-learning hours.

Ideally, Barry wants to be a good husband, father, employee, and student. These conflicting roles have created a dilemma that is not easily resolved. Ultimately, Barry decides to make the best of a difficult situation.

Step 6: Evaluate and Reflect on the Decision

Barry resents what he considers to be an additional burden and feels that he is being forced to participate in an activity that places added demands on his already stressful life. He is concerned about how all this extra work will affect his wife and child. He is not sure he can sustain such a rigorous schedule throughout the semester without adversely affecting his health, family, and grades.

Barry is unwilling to drop his minor, because fluency in Spanish will help him with community relations and help him to become a better employee and social worker. Neither selecting two substitute courses nor dropping this course are viable options for Barry. He is reluctant to delay graduation and change his goals with so few courses left to graduate. And, Barry and his wife agree that reducing his work hours and incurring more debt will only add stress to their already demanding budget.

Despite the potential negative consequences, Barry remains committed to his program of study and is willing to make the sacrifice if it helps him become a better social worker. In addition, he has frequently felt disengaged from the younger students in his class and hopes this experience will help him feel more connected to other students and to the college. He reflects on how he would explain this decision to his child someday and clearly sees the long-term benefits. Barry is, however, unsure about participating in community service in the future because of the hardship he will endure this semester.

In the process of resolving this dilemma, though, Barry has gained experience in ethical decision-making and dealing with competing demands and courses of action. He recognizes that in the world of work he may be faced with contradictory decisions and behaviors and will, therefore, need to use critical thinking strategies to deal with clients, referral services, community, state and federal regulations, and the legal system. Barry vows that, whatever the situation, he will be respectful and responsible and will consider the perspectives of all parties to provide clients and families with the best and most useful solutions to their problems and dilemmas.

In sum, when applying the pillow, newspaper, and child tests, Barry is satisfied with his course of action. With the support of his family and recognition of the long-term benefits of his decision, he will be able to sleep comfortably. He would be pleased to have his story of commitment and motivation published in the local newspaper and would have no problem explaining to his children the worthiness of the choices he made.

Related Issues

The demographics of the typical college student are changing as a larger number of nontraditional students are attending colleges and universities to earn undergraduate and graduate degrees. These students are usually 25 years of age or older and are working full time, supporting aging parents, and often raising children. This case provides an example of the ethical dilemmas faced by nontraditional students on a daily basis. They often make difficult choices and decisions as they attempt to meet work, family, and school demands. Engaging in yet another activity can create an additional burden. Instructors are, therefore, faced with difficult decisions as they structure course requirements to provide the best and most effective learning experience for all students. Is it realistic to expect someone who is working and supporting a family to not only spend long hours studying but also to engage in service in the community? Should course requirements be adjusted for the nontraditional student? What are college and university faculty and administrators' responsibilities for the quality of education for the nontraditional student? Can and should we make accommodations? Service-learning is based on university, community, and individual common good or benefit. If this is the case, are we overlooking or ignoring the personal good of these nontraditional students in order to accomplish public good?

Additional Dilemma

Sarah is a new student in a psychology program at a local college. She is returning to school after raising her children and anxiously attends her first class. She is dismayed to find that her introductory psychology course has a service-learning component at a local nonprofit agency for inner-city, at-risk youth. Sarah is on the executive advisory board for another similar agency in the community. Both agencies and their boards have been competing over the last five years for limited community resources.

Sarah has enjoyed her community activities for over 15 years and believes this service-learning component will be useful to the agency and the students. In addition, she wants to do well in all her classes and in particular her first class. However, she is unsure how her agency would view her participation in this community service. Would they consider her a traitor for helping a competing agency? Would the class-designated agency think of her as a spy?

Sarah is hesitant about talking to her professor, since he seems committed to this activity and eager to have the students participate. She does not want to be viewed as a difficult student and is unwilling to question her professor's authority and the course requirements.

1) Identify the ethical dilemma.

2) Why is it an ethical dilemma? Identify the relevant codes.

3) Identify and list information you think would be helpful in making a decision.

4) List at least three possible solutions to this dilemma.

5) Which of the proposed solutions would you choose?

6) Why would you choose this solution?

7) How would you evaluate whether this is a good solution?

Chapter Five

Confidentiality and Student Responsibility to Agency

Julie, a 20-year-old psychology major and a junior at a local university, is involved in her first service-learning course. The course is Human Development and the service-learning project involves understanding the impact of poverty at different stages of development. Julie is a commuter student who lives with her parents in a very small residential neighborhood near the university. Her immediate and extended families are very close and have been residents of the community for several generations. Julie hopes to continue her education and become a master's-level counselor who works with children and families. She has chosen a homeless shelter as the site of her service-learning project. The shelter provides many services that help families in need maintain their family unit. It also operates a food bank that is open to all members of the community. In order to participate in all aspects of the services provided by the shelter, Julie spends a day in the food bank.

In an attempt to meet the needs of the community, the food bank provides emergency food supplements to needy individuals and families, and is designed to aid those who have left the shelter and are now living independently in the community. While at the food bank, Julie encounters a situation that she is totally unprepared to handle. She sees her Uncle Ed enter the food bank to obtain a week's supply of food. Her uncle makes eye contact with her, but doesn't approach her or make any effort to talk with her. Julie is sure that he not only saw her, but recognized her as well. She is too surprised to do anything but stare in disbelief. Uncle Ed stands in line with the other recipients, takes the bag of food that is offered to him, and leaves. Julie is confused and angry. She questions whether to tell her family about Uncle Ed's visit to the food bank. Does Uncle Ed need help? Certainly her family would provide all the help he needs. She is angry because Uncle Ed does not seem to need financial help. He lives in a very nice house, buys a new car every other year, and seems financially secure. What is he doing at a food bank?

First and foremost, is there an ethical dilemma? What should Julie do? What is Julie's responsibility to the food bank? To her uncle? To her family? What ethical principles apply to this situation?

Step 1: Identify and Define the Dilemma

Using the structure proposed in Chapter 2 for the ethical decision-making process, Julie needs to consider several factors. She is faced with a dilemma that arose from multiple and competing goals. Julie is torn between her duty to *treat service recipients in a manner consistent with ethical principles* (SLC I.4), her responsibility to *adhere to the policies and procedures of the community agency* (SLC I.3), and her personal desire to inform her family that a family member is in need (SLC I.7). She is also concerned that her uncle may be cheating the system and utilizing scarce resources that may be desperately needed by other members of the community.

Step 2: Address Relevant Principles and Gather Information

Julie's initial reactions are a very important factor in this situation. Julie is too stunned to do anything when she observes her uncle. Julie wants to tell her family about seeing Uncle Ed at the food bank. She knows that they would be very willing to help Uncle Ed if he were truly in need. She feels personally conflicted about her responsibility to her uncle and other family members. She also wants to tell the director of the food bank that Uncle Ed is taking resources from families that are in greater need. She realizes that she is experiencing a range of very strong conflicting emotions that include anger, surprise, and confusion.

Julie's first task is to do nothing until she is able to make some sense of her own reactions to this situation. The fact that she was too surprised to respond when she saw her uncle at the food bank was probably the best-case scenario, because it gave Julie the time she needed to carefully consider her options. Had she approached her uncle in the food bank, she may have experienced unintended consequences, such as embarrassing him unnecessarily or creating an unpleasant scene for both of them. There may be valid reasons for her uncle's appearance that have nothing to do with her initial assumptions or reactions. For instance, her uncle might be picking up the bag of food for a neighbor or friend who has no transportation. So Julie must decide if she is overreacting to this situation or if there is an actual ethical issue that needs to be resolved and addressed.

Next, Julie needs to consider what ethical principles apply to this case. The primary issue in this case is one of confidentiality, which involves the principle of autonomy and respect for people's rights. Does Julie's uncle have a right to privacy and confidentiality? Does Julie have any legal or ethical responsibility to respect her uncle's privacy and maintain his right to confidentiality? What is Julie's obligation because of her status as a student representing the university? If Uncle Ed is acting unethically by taking food (resources) from others, does Julie have a responsibility to tell the director of the center?

A more troubling ethical issue, stemming from the ethical principles for service-learning experiences, involves the issue of justice, specifically the fair use of scarce resources. Julie knows that the food bank is not able to provide for the needs of all the individuals who line up outside the doors for food. When the food runs out, people are turned away. Julie does not perceive her uncle as needy and she knows that Uncle Ed's family would gladly assist him if they knew of his plight. It is her perception that Uncle Ed is taking food from others who need it more than he.

Who can help Julie with this situation? The agency director is certainly one resource. Julie can propose a hypothetical situation to the director to maintain her uncle's privacy at this point in the discussion. Through this consultation, Julie would discover if the food bank has a policy of confidentiality or privacy that applies to the people it serves and if the agency has specific criteria based on need. If so, Julie is faced with the reality that her uncle may actually meet the need criteria. If the food bank does not have specific need criteria, then Uncle's Ed's behavior may be selfish, but totally permissible by the standards of the food bank. Uncle Ed may not be living by the equity principle of justice and fairness, and his actions may be harmful to others, but Julie is unable to intervene without violating her responsibility to adhere to the policies of the agency. Julie is faced with many ethical issues and needs to sort them out.

The faculty member would be an excellent choice for consultation. The faculty member has an ethical obligation to the agency and needs to provide adequate supervision to the student to ensure the agency's right to confidentiality. However, many faculty members do not consider themselves equipped to handle strong emotional reactions and personal conflicts such as the ones Julie is experiencing. In planning a service-learning experience, members of the faculty need to consider the wide range of possible consequences that community involvement may produce. The professor should help Julie through this situation or refer her to another professional who would be able to help her sort out her conflicting emotions.

In addition to the SLC, the American Psychological Association's (APA) Ethical Principles of Psychologists and Code of Conduct is applicable in this case. As a psychology student, Julie needs to be aware of the guidelines for professional behavior that are provided by the relevant professional organizations. This is certainly an issue Julie can explore in her service-learning reflection papers. The reflections may help her identify, clarify, and analyze her reactions and the ethical issues involved. An additional reflection activity might be a class discussion of ethical issues students encounter while participating in their service-learning experiences. Thus all students in the class may learn vicariously through a discussion of Julie's experience.

Step 3: Propose Courses of Action

The next step in the process of ethical decision-making would provide Julie with the opportunity to explore the range of options available to her. Julie might decide to:

- *Action A:* Say nothing to anyone about her uncle.

- *Action B:* Confront her uncle directly.

- *Action C:* Discuss the situation with her family.

- *Action D:* Maintain her uncle's right to confidentiality after consultation.

Step 4: Determine and Analyze the Consequences for Each Proposed Course of Action

Action A: Say nothing to anyone about her uncle.

Positive. If Julie decides to keep this information to herself, she is choosing to maintain her uncle's right to confidentiality, and she is respecting his right to autonomy.

Negative. The negative consequence is that Julie must then deal with the range of conflicting emotions she is experiencing, and this may impair her ability to function effectively in class and at the homeless shelter. She may be afraid of seeing her uncle a second time. Another problem with this option is that while Julie might be able to maintain her uncle's "secret," she may not be able to fulfill her responsibility to the agency. As a student, she has a responsibility to *adhere to the policies and procedures of the agency* (SLC I.3), and such policies may require her to report any suspected fraud.

Action B: Confront her uncle directly.

Positive. Julie may still be troubled that her uncle is cheating the system. After consulting with her college and onsite supervisors, Julie may find that it is acceptable for her to confront her uncle. The positive consequence of this action is that Julie is able to discuss her conflicting emotions directly with her uncle, and possibly feel better that she has vented her frustrations.

Negative. While an honest confrontation would be the most direct intervention, a negative consequence might be the unintended embarrassment and/or alienation of her uncle.

Action C: Discuss the situation with her family.

Positive. If Julie decides to discuss the situation with her family, she may feel better about "getting it off her chest," and this may seem like a positive consequence for Julie.

Negative. Julie could be violating the policies and procedures of the agency and her uncle's right to confidentiality. This is often one of the most difficult lessons for students in human service professions. The concept of confidentiality often means keeping information from spouses and family. An academic service-learning experience is an excellent opportunity for students to practice this skill.

Action D: Maintain her uncle's right to confidentiality after consultation.

    Positive. Julie will maintain her uncle's right to confidentiality after consultation with her supervisors. Julie has received support from her supervisors and she can use them as a resource for discussing any lingering negative feelings she may have. If another situation with her uncle arises in the agency, her supervisors will be aware of the circumstances and they will be in a better position to handle the situation or help Julie through it.

    Negative. An unintended negative consequence of this course of action involves Julie personally. She feels embarrassed about her uncle's situation and finds it difficult to share this "secret" with her supervisors. She also has to determine how she will manage her feelings when she sees her uncle at a family event.

Step 5: Decide on the Best Course of Action

Julie's best course of action appears to be Action D. With this option she abides by the SLC as well as the ethical guidelines of the American Psychological Association. She has used the process of consultation to help clarify her responsibilities and has learned a valuable lesson about confidentiality in the helping profession.

Step 6: Evaluate and Reflect on the Decision

Julie's decision to maintain her uncle's right to confidentiality is probably in her uncle's best interest. It may be the best solution in terms of the ethical principles of autonomy and respect for people's rights, which involve issues of confidentiality, but Julie may have unresolved questions about her uncle's use of scarce resources. Using the pillow test to evaluate this decision, Julie finds herself wrestling with some sleepless nights when she thinks of needy people in the community who may be denied resources because of her uncle's behavior. She understands the need to keep information confidential, but she is beginning to realize that these decisions are very complicated and may involve personal distress. Julie is comfortable with her decision when it is put to the newspaper test. Julie finds herself wondering about how a child might evaluate her action.

Related Issues

This case raises another issue that involves the development of ethical reasoning skills through service-learning experiences. As suggested earlier, the APA code of ethics can be used as a guide in this situation. It is uncertain at what point during the preparation of an undergraduate student of psychology the APA and the APA code of ethics should be introduced. The code of ethics is mentioned in introductory psychology courses during discussions of ethical practice in research, but more practice-oriented aspects of the code may not be introduced until a senior-level internship course.

While membership in the APA commits members to adhere to the APA code, nonmembership does not absolve students from the duty to be aware of the code and responsibility to abide by it in the practice of the profession. Since Julie is enrolled in a psychology course and practicing in the field, the APA code is a good place to begin to search for guidelines. It would be the faculty member's responsibility to prepare Julie for the service-learning experience by providing her with applicable APA code of ethics guidelines before she begins her service-learning experience. This does not mean that every course should examine every aspect of a professional code. However, professional codes of ethics can be incorporated into the course content of a service-learning course when instructors provide code guidelines specific to the experience. Julie, as a psychology student, should have been made aware of the APA code as a guide to behavior. This raises the general question of whether students in all disciplines need to be educated about the professional code of ethics much earlier in their formal undergraduate experience.

Additional Dilemma

A computer information course with a service-learning component has students install programs on the computers of a nonprofit community service agency. While installing a program, a student discovers information about a family member stored on the computer. This is sensitive information about a health condition of the family member, and the student is certain that no one in the family is aware of this information. Since the health condition is potentially contagious, the student is conflicted about his responsibility to keep his family safe and his responsibility to maintain the confidentiality of the information he garners through his work as a computer specialist.

1) Identify the ethical dilemma.

2) Why is it an ethical dilemma? Identify the relevant codes.

3) Identify and list information you think would be helpful in making a decision.

4) List at least three possible solutions to this dilemma.

5) Which of the proposed solutions would you choose?

6) Why would you choose this solution?

7) How would you evaluate whether this is a good solution?

Chapter Six

Research and Informed Consent

J essica is a senior biology major who is completing a service-learning
project for a capstone course in her program. The project involves
developing a hands-on biology class activity for a class of seventh-grade
students in a general science classroom. The students in this class have
been working on science fair projects for six months. The projects are
nearly complete when Jessica begins her service-learning project. As she
spends the first week of this assignment observing the classroom, she has
no role in the design of the projects. The projects are all presented at a science fair exhibition where professors from local colleges and universities
judge the entries and determine which projects will be entered in a regional competition. One student in Jessica's classroom has been chosen to
enter his project in the next level of competition. The student is excited
about this recognition and is eager to compete. The supervising teacher
asks Jessica to spend some extra time with this student to help him prepare
his project for the competition. Jessica, an avid researcher in her undergraduate program, gladly accepts the task.

The teacher gives Jessica the list of regulations for the competition. In
reviewing the project with the student, Jessica realizes that the student's
research, which tested the claims of two different whitening toothpastes,
involved human participants. In designing the project, the student had
not prepared an informed consent form for the participants or obtained
any type of written consent from them, their parents, or the school officials. The rules for the regional competition clearly state that documented
informed consent is necessary for any project that involves human participants. Jessica brings this to the attention of the classroom teacher who
supervised the original research. The teacher tells Jessica that she did not
review the rules for the regional competition before approving the student's project. She also tells Jessica that "it's only a seventh-grade science

fair project," and instructs her to make up an informed consent form and have her friends sign the names of the participants so that the paperwork will be in order and the student will be able to enter his project into the competition.

What should Jessica do? Is there an ethical dilemma in this situation? What is Jessica's responsibility to the student? To the supervising teacher? To the college she represents? What ethical principles apply to this situation?

Step 1: Identify and Define the Dilemma

Despite her best intentions of completing a service-learning assignment, Jessica has stumbled upon a complex situation that she is now forced to manage. SLC I.3 states that *students must adhere to the policies and procedures of the community agency*, yet SLC I.6 states that the *student agrees to abide by any applicable legal and ethical guidelines.* As a senior biology student, Jessica was involved in many research projects under the supervision of her college faculty. She learned the appropriate ethical guidelines for conducting research, especially those that pertain to the protection of human participants in research. Jessica knows that these ethical guidelines require informed consent prior to the beginning of research that involves human subjects. She also knows that as part of her service-learning contract with the school, she agreed to accept tasks assigned to her by the supervising teacher. However, she never anticipated that an assigned task might involve deceptive and potentially fraudulent activity, especially in a seventh-grade classroom. Jessica does not want to defy the supervising teacher, nor does she want the student to have to withdraw his project from the competition. But she is very uncomfortable with signing fake consent forms.

Step 2: Address Relevant Principles and Gather Information

Jessica's uneasiness in this situation is a testament to the quality of the research training she received in her biology program. To resolve this issue, Jessica needs to evaluate the relevant ethical principles, the ethical guidelines of service-learning, and her role in this situation with respect to the ethics of conducting research.

First, Jessica needs to consider the ethical principles that apply to this case. A primary issue is one of autonomy and respect for people's rights. The participants in this study were denied the right to be informed of the risks and benefits of the research, but more importantly, they were denied the right to refuse to participate in the research. The teacher now asks Jessica to compound the problem by faking signatures after the fact. This deception affects the integrity of the research, as well as Jessica's personal sense of integrity. Jessica is also faced with the potential legal issues involved in forging signatures.

Jessica does not want to defy the teacher's instructions. She is, after all, a guest in this teacher's classroom. However, she cannot bring herself to ignore the potential legal and ethical implications of the teacher's directive. As she is unsure of which course of action to follow, Jessica's next step is to seek supervision.

Who can help Jessica with this situation? The most logical choice is her course instructor. The instructor and Jessica could together brainstorm possible solutions. Jessica finds herself in this unexpected situation because of the course's service-learning assignment. Clearly, the faculty has prepared Jessica in the ethics of conducting research, because she readily recognized the issues involved. In planning a service-learning experience, instructors need to consider the wide range of consequences that community involvement may produce, though this one would have been very difficult to predict.

The service-learning reflection papers would be a good tool to use for contemplating the issues. The reflection exercises may help Jessica identify, clarify, and analyze her reactions as well as the ethical and legal issues involved. Jessica continues to ponder the teacher's statement, "It's only a seventh-grade science fair project." She questions the point at which the ethical standards of research apply. Is it really appropriate to expect seventh-graders to be trained in the ethical conduct of research? Yet the guidelines provided for the regional competition require compliance with the highest ethical standards for research. Jessica's dilemma might present an excellent opportunity for class discussion and additional input from classmates.

Step 3: Propose Courses of Action

The next step in the process of ethical decision-making would give Jessica the opportunity to explore the range of available options:

- *Action A:* Comply with the teacher's directive to fake the signatures on the informed consent form, but explain to the student that this action is unethical.

- *Action B:* Confront the teacher directly with her concerns.

- *Action C:* Refuse to comply with the teacher's directive.

- *Action D:* Request that the college instructor intervene.

- *Action E:* Ask participants to complete the informed consent forms after the fact.

Step 4: Determine and Analyze the Consequences for Each Proposed Course of Action

Action A: Comply with the teacher's directive to fake the signatures on the informed consent form, but explain to the student that this action is unethical.

Positive. This may be the easiest solution, because Jessica's compliance will ensure that she is able to maintain a positive relationship with the supervising teacher and be able to complete the rest of her service-learning requirement without conflict. The seventh-grade student will also be able to enter his project in the county competition, and Jessica will be satisfied that she has explained to the student that this is not the proper way to conduct research.

Negative. The negative consequence is that Jessica must then deal with the damage to her own integrity and the potential legal issues involved in the faking of signatures. As a student, she has a *responsibility to adhere to the policies and procedures of the agency* (SLC I.3), and such policies may require her to report any suspected fraud to the principal. Telling the student that this is not the proper way to conduct research may cause the student to lose respect for his teacher and compromise the teacher's ability to be effective in the classroom. The student may take from this experience the idea that the end justifies the means and that unethical behavior is acceptable if it resolves the problem in his favor.

Action B: Confront the teacher directly with her concerns.

Positive. After consulting with her college instructor, Jessica may decide to confront the teacher directly with her concerns about faking signatures. The supervising teacher may not have realized all of the implications of her initial decision. If an open and honest discussion occurs in an atmosphere of mutual respect, the teacher may agree with Jessica's concerns. As a consequence, the seventh-grade student would have to be told that he could not enter his project into the competition. The student could learn a powerful lesson about the ethical conduct of research. It could be an opportunity for Jessica to learn to be diplomatic, yet assertive, when confronting a supervisor.

Negative. While an honest confrontation would be the most direct intervention, a negative consequence might be the unintended embarrassment and/or alienation of the supervising teacher. This may strain the relationship between Jessica and the teacher and make it difficult for Jessica to complete her service-learning requirement. If the teacher does agree with Jessica's assessment of the situation, it also means that the seventh-grade student must be told that he cannot enter his project into the research competition. This will undoubtedly result in great disappointment, as he is very excited that he was chosen for the next round of competition. The student may experience feelings of mistrust toward his teacher and begin to question the rules, directions, and advice she provides. Another unintended consequence might be a hostile reaction from the student's parents if they are not tactfully informed of the reasons for the decision. If the teacher does not agree with Jessica's assessment of the situation, she may again direct Jessica to fake the informed-consent form despite her ethical objections. Jessica would then be faced with another difficult decision.

Action C: Refuse to comply with the teacher's directive.

Positive. If Jessica simply refuses to comply with the teacher's directive without any direct discussion of the issues involved, she is cleared of responsibility and her ethical dilemma is resolved.

Negative. While Jessica's refusal to comply may remove her from the situation and from any ethical responsibility, it will probably result in a negative reaction from the supervising teacher and a potentially antagonistic relationship. This may impact Jessica's ability to complete the rest of her service-learning requirements. It may also result in a strained or ruptured relationship with the community school. Students in service-learning situations are not acting as independent agents. Instead, they must *behave as professional representatives of the college/university at all times* (SLC 1.1). This can be a difficult lesson to learn. An academic service-learning experience is an excellent opportunity for students to develop an understanding of the broader implications of their choices and behaviors.

Another negative consequence of this course of action might be that the supervising teacher then fakes the signatures on the informed consent form and never really understands the ethical and legal implications of her decision. It is possible that this teacher has not been trained in the ethics of research and the opportunity to educate her will be lost. One of the advantages of the service-learning experience is that both the community agency (or school) and the student involved in the experience will derive equivalent benefits. This is clearly a situation in which the student may take on the role of teacher/advisor/consultant and share her knowledge and expertise in the ethics of research with the supervising teacher. If the teacher does decide to fake the signatures, and Jessica becomes aware of the situation, she would again be faced with a decision to inform the principal or remain silent.

Action D: Request that the college instructor intervene.

Positive. Intervention by the college instructor takes the responsibility for the situation away from Jessica. Thus, she is not placed in the situation of having to confront a supervising teacher and then deal with the potentially negative reactions by herself. SLC II.2 recognizes faculty responsibility to *minimize potential harm to agencies, their constituents, and students.* The college instructor's intervention would allow the inevitable discussion of research ethics to occur between professionals of comparable status.

Negative. A negative consequence of this course of action involves Jessica personally. While it might be appropriate for the college instructor to intervene, Jessica is denied the opportunity to practice asserting her position with a supervisor and clearly articulating and defending her moral/ethical/legal convictions regarding this situation.

Action E: Ask participants to complete the informed consent form after the fact.

Positive. Because the study was testing the effects of whitening toothpaste by photographing teeth during the project, it might be safe to assume that the participants and their guardians had given implied consent. Asking the participants to sign an informed consent form after the fact might be an acceptable option. It would provide a learning opportunity for the student researcher and the participants. The student would be able to comply with the county regulations and enter his project in the contest.

Negative. Because the informed consent was not properly administered, the actual purpose of informed consent is negated. Participants were not told ahead of time of any risks associated with the study, that they could withdraw at any time, and that their participation was strictly voluntary. This option might also leave students with the impression that obtaining informed consent after the fact is an acceptable research practice.

Step 5: Decide on the Best Course of Action

While none of the proposed courses of action presents an ideal solution to this dilemma, Jessica's best course of action appears to be Action B. Through this choice of action, she is able to maintain her service-learning agreement to *abide by any applicable legal and ethical guidelines* (SLC I.6) and to *behave as a professional representative of the college/university at all times* (SLC I.1). The act of confronting the supervising teacher alone does not resolve the situation, but it does provide the opportunity for more dialogue with the supervising teacher about the complicated issues involved. Ideally, Jessica and the supervising teacher will be able to discuss the situation in depth with the seventh-grade student and his parents. Jessica also learns to tactfully confront a supervisor and clearly state her position. This is a situation where the student may take on the role of teacher/advisor/consultant and share her knowledge and expertise in the ethics of research with the supervising teacher. She has used the process of consultation to help clarify her responsibilities and both she and the college instructor have learned a valuable lesson about expecting the unexpected in service-learning situations. One of the advantages of the service-learning experience is that everyone involved in the experience derives equivalent benefits.

Step 6: Evaluate and Reflect on the Decision

Jessica's decision to confront the teacher directly with her concerns was not an easy decision, nor did it fully resolve the situation involving the seventh-grade student's research project. It is an example of how the best course of action in a complicated situation may only be the first step in the process of finding a solution. A complete resolution would require the involvement of the seventh-grade student, his parents, the supervising teacher, Jessica, and possibly the school principal. It is not an easy decision, because it would probably necessitate an admission from the supervising teacher that she was unaware of the guidelines for conducting research with human participants, and more specifically that she was unaware of the rules of the county competition. It might also mean that the seventh-grade student would not be able to enter his project into the county competition. Clearly, Jessica's action affects others. It illustrates the principle of nonmaleficence, where even the best course of action may have some negative effects.

Using the pillow test to evaluate her decision, Jessica has some sleepless nights as she thinks of the effects on the supervising teacher and the seventh-grade student. However, she believes that the newspaper test validates her decision. She would not want the local newspaper to print a lead story about how she forged the signatures of research participants. Using the child test, Jessica is comfortable that because "it's only a seventh-grade science fair project," it is exactly the right time to stress the ethics of research and to teach a child that the end may not always justify the means.

Related Issues

The complicated situation presented in this case highlights the need for continuous discussion of ethics and ethical principles. The ethical principles presented in Chapter 1 are not mutually exclusive, nor are they presented in a hierarchal fashion. Each ethical dilemma must be considered with respect to all the principles and their interrelatedness. The overriding principle in one situation might not take precedence in another. In this case, the principles of nonmaleficence and integrity are paramount, but Jessica is probably violating the principle of fidelity by challenging the teacher's instructions. The best decision often involves a solution that considers the interests and well-being of others as having as much importance as one's own well-being.

This case raises issues about ethics in research, when and where the ethics in research are taught, and the responsibility of colleges and universities to provide instruction in ethics to elementary science teachers. These teachers may be well trained in elementary teaching techniques but less well prepared in science research methodology. The case also raises questions about the community school's responsibility to provide in-service training to its teachers on issues related to ethical teaching practices.

An equally important related issue is the responsibility of school systems (preschool through post-graduate) to foster moral development. Morality in the broadest sense involves values, relationships with others, and judgments about right and wrong (Ehrlich, 2003). Education in the United States is committed to the promotion of democratic values, good judgment, and a strong moral compass. In this scenario there are at least three different parties involved: Jessica, the seventh-grade student, and the supervising teacher. Each of them might be functioning at a different level of moral development. The reasoning process that occurs at each level will affect the decision each party makes. This scenario provides the opportunity for the deliberate consideration of a complex moral and ethical dilemma where informed judgments are translated into sound, responsible action.

Additional Dilemma

Tom is a nursing student involved in a service-learning research project through his advanced nursing leadership course. The research involves administering a survey to patients who have been diagnosed with terminal cancer. The survey is also administered to their spouses. The site supervisor, concerned about the size of the sample, suggests that the student go to each hospital room to ask the patients to participate. "In this way," says the supervisor, "it will be easier to get participants to comply." Tom approaches Mrs. Yung, an Asian immigrant, while her husband is away from the unit for treatment. Mrs. Yung agrees to participate in the study, and tells Tom that her husband would also like to participate, but that he does not know that he has a terminal illness and that she does not want him to know. She tells Tom that in her culture, it would be considered a burden for the patient to have the information about his illness. What should Tom do?

1) Identify the ethical dilemma.

2) Why is it an ethical dilemma? Identify the relevant codes.

3) Identify and list information you think would be helpful in making a decision.

4) List at least three possible solutions to this dilemma.

5) Which of the proposed solutions would you choose?

6) Why would you choose this solution?

7) How would you evaluate whether this is a good solution?

Chapter Seven

Treating Service Recipients With Respect and Understanding Assignment Limitations

Nathan is a first-year nursing major who has registered for an elective course, "Contemporary Religions." The theology course has a service-learning course component in which students interview residents of a local nursing home to develop an oral history of their faith journeys. In partial completion of his assignment, Nathan is required to spend at least 20 hours interviewing and socializing with one resident throughout the semester. Nathan has developed a close relationship with his resident partner and often spends several hours each weekend with him. On one of these weekend visits, the resident's daughter is also visiting. As she is leaving, she pulls Nathan aside and whispers, "My dad loves candy, but you know that he's diabetic and shouldn't have any sweets. Please don't give him candy if he asks." Nathan is surprised, because although he is a nursing major and has been studying the effects of diabetes, he had never considered the fact that his resident might have any serious dietary restrictions. Nathan has seen the resident munching on candy bars in his room on several occasions, and he has observed the resident asking other residents to get him a regular (not diet) cola from the vending machine.

Later in the semester, after spending several pleasant hours together, Nathan is about to leave for the day when the resident asks him to retrieve a small paper bag from his dresser. Nathan complies with the request, but as he grabs the bag, it opens and the contents spill out. The bag is full of chocolate candy bars that the resident has hidden. Nathan remembers the daughter's admonition. Is there an ethical dilemma in this situation? What should Nathan do?

Step 1: Identify and Define the Dilemma

Nathan is faced with a difficult decision. He has a good relationship with this resident and respects the man's opinions. Although Nathan is spending time in the nursing home because of a service-learning requirement in a theology class, his nursing classes have given him an elementary understanding of diabetes and the medical complications that can occur with this disease. The resident is waiting for the candy and Nathan has only an instant to make a decision. He feels conflicted over his desire to *treat service recipients in a manner consistent with ethical principles* (SLC I.4) and the sudden realization that *students in service learning shall understand their role and its limitations in the context of the service-learning assignment* (SLC I.2) and *abide by applicable legal and ethical guidelines* (SLC I.6). Nathan feels ill-equipped to handle this situation. He questions whether he, as a student in a theology class who has developed a friendship with this resident, has the legal, ethical, or moral responsibility to deny the man his bag of candy. He wonders if the resident actually does have dietary restrictions, given his own observations of the resident eating candy and drinking cola. Nathan also wonders what will happen to the man if he truly is diabetic and he consumes a large quantity of candy bars. Nathan clearly does not know the limits of his duties and responsibilities in this situation. In the few moments he has to make a decision, he realizes that he is acting as a representative of the college. He wonders if he can ignore his own understanding of the physical effects of a serious medical condition and still act as a responsible nursing student. Is it ethically permissible to give the man the candy knowing that there could be serious health consequences? But can he deny this man the right to make his own choices, even if they are potentially harmful? Does Nathan become an accomplice in this resident's unhealthy choices if he hands the man the bag of candy?

Step 2: Address Relevant Principles and Gather Information

Timing is an important issue in this case. Nathan doesn't have a lot of time to gather information. Yet he does have options.

As mentioned earlier, a relevant ethical principle in this case involves autonomy and respect for people's rights. Although the resident lives in a nursing home, he is not cognitively incapacitated, nor has he been identified as incompetent to make his own decisions. He is an 85-year-old man who is physically handicapped from a stroke but not mentally debilitated. He resides in the nursing home because of his compromised physical condition. The ethical principle of autonomy requires acknowledging that this man continues to have the cognitive capacity to choose his own destiny—even if it means that he makes poor choices: The resident may be harming his own health, and in doing so may increase the amount of care he requires at the nursing home. While this may not be considered a matter of physical harm to others, it may increase the cost of care for all the residents.

Nathan also realizes that the ethical principle of nonmaleficence applies in this situation. Nathan wants to protect this man from harm, and he does not want to contribute to the man's deteriorating physical health. Nathan is faced with a classic ethical struggle of deciding which ethical principle takes priority.

Unfortunately, Nathan does not have the luxury of time to consult with the theology professor supervising this service-learning project. At best, he can attempt to find and consult with a member of the nursing home staff. But he is still faced with a bag of candy and the resident who is waiting for it.

Step 3: Propose Courses of Action

In the brief amount of time that he has to consider his options, Nathan considers three alternatives:

- *Action A:* Give the candy to the resident.

- *Action B:* Take the bag of candy to the nurses' station.

- *Action C:* Confront the resident about the candy.

Step 4: Determine and Analyze the Consequences for Each Proposed Course of Action

Action A: Give the candy to the resident.

Positive. Nathan can simply hand over the bag of candy and allow the resident to make his own decisions about what, when, and how much to eat. With this option, Nathan is able to remove himself from the conflict and can justify his action, because he has not obstructed the resident's autonomy in making his own decisions and coping with the consequences of those decisions. Nathan can also justify this decision because he is acting as a service-learning participant in a theology course, not as a nursing student. Nathan will not be compromising his positive relationship with the resident through this action.

Negative. The negative consequences of this choice are significant. The resident may experience serious medical complications from consuming large amounts of sugar. Nathan is likely to experience significant ethical and emotional distress as he considers the potential consequences of his actions.

Action B: Take the bag of candy to the nurses' station.

Positive. Nathan could choose to take the candy to the nurses' station and completely remove the potentially harmful items from the resident. The resident is then protected from his own poor choices, and Nathan is acting within the ethical standards of his chosen profession.

Negative. This action is paternalistic in that Nathan presumes to know what is best for the resident and denies the resident the right to make autonomous choices. It is likely that Nathan's relationship with the resident will suffer as a result of this decision.

Action C: Confront the resident about the candy.

Positive. Nathan can maintain the resident's right to autonomy by addressing the issue directly with the resident. The principle of autonomy requires that an individual has access to the information necessary to make a rational, informed decision. If Nathan chooses to discuss the issue with the resident, he can reconcile his distress about his nursing-student role versus his theology-student role and provide the resident with factual information about the dangers of uncontrolled diabetes.

Negative. Nathan may feel less emotional distress if he has a discussion with the resident about the dangers of candy consumption, but the resident may still choose to eat the candy. Thus, the potentially negative consequences of Action A could be repeated because of this decision.

Step 5: Decide on the Best Course of Action

While none of the proposed courses of action presents an ideal solution to this dilemma, Nathan's best course of action appears to be Action C. Through this choice of action, he is able to maintain his service-learning agreement to *abide by applicable legal and ethical guidelines* (SLC I.6) and *understand his role and its limitations in the context of the service-learning assignment* (SLC I.2). The act of confronting the resident does not resolve the situation, but it provides the opportunity for more dialogue between Nathan and the resident. Nathan preserves the resident's right to autonomy. In his discussion with the resident, Nathan could use his knowledge of the negative health effects of diabetes to educate the resident, thus practicing one of the important roles of a nursing student. Nathan could also encourage the resident to give the candy to the nurse himself, thus involving the resident in the decision in a very active way. If Nathan's educational message and his persuasive techniques fail, he might choose to follow up this course of action by handing over the candy to the resident or reporting the candy incident to the nurse on duty.

Step 6: Evaluate and Reflect on the Decision

Nathan's decision to discuss the situation with the resident directly was not an easy one, nor did it resolve the situation completely. It illustrates the conflict between two ethical principles, autonomy and nonmaleficence, and the SLC, in which even the best course of action may have some negative effects.

Using the pillow test as an evaluation of this decision, Nathan finds himself still distressed because he could not prevent a potentially harmful situation from occurring. He is facing a conflict that he will see time and again in his role as a health care professional. Even under the best of circumstances, individuals make poor choices that are harmful to their health. This may cause some sleepless nights, but Nathan is going to have to resolve this issue, because he will face it again.

Nathan is unsure if he would like to see his decision on the front page of the newspaper. Using the newspaper test, Nathan realizes that he judges himself as not having done enough in this situation, and feels that he would be negatively judged by others as well. Using the child test, Nathan is again uncomfortable with his decision, because he would have preferred the decision to be more straightforward. He would have appreciated a clearer right-versus-wrong distinction if he had to explain it to a child.

Related Issues

In this situation, it is possible that Nathan could change his mind about his decision after consulting with his professor. Whatever was decided in this case may not have been ideal, but one must rely on the resources at hand when faced with having to make a decision on the spot. Nathan might have to return to the nursing home and address the issue again with the resident and the medical staff. Being confronted with having to right an apparent wrong is an uncomfortable situation for anyone, but the role of student provides the opportunity to practice living according to one's moral and ethical convictions. It is also important for students to realize that faculty and supervisors are generally forgiving when mistakes are openly addressed and shortcomings readily admitted.

The level of personal discomfort Nathan experiences as a result of this situation is an important related issue. With good supervision, Nathan may come to appreciate that he will face many similar dilemmas in his role as a heath care provider. If this situation is not resolved in a manner that preserves Nathan's confidence and dignity, then his desire to participate in future service-learning activities may decline.

Additional Dilemma

Jane, an honor student and second-year physics major, is enrolled in a "Perspectives in Education" course. She decides to take the class to satisfy a general education elective and to help her decide if teaching could be in her future. She believes this course will give her the experience and knowledge she needs to make an informed decision about changing her major to education.

As part of the requirement for the course, students become pen pals with elementary students at two local schools. Jane has developed a writing relationship with Sarah, a third grader. Sarah confides in Jane that her mother leaves her and her younger sister alone for periods of time, particularly at night. Sarah writes that she really loves her mother and does not want to hurt her, but is upset that she is solely responsible for her sister during these times and that sometimes it is "pretty scary at night."

Jane is not quite sure what to do with this information. If she tells her instructor, she believes she will violate the relationship she has developed with the child. With her limited understanding of child endangerment, Jane is unsure whether this is really a problem or not. How should Jane proceed? What are her responsibilities to Sarah?

1) Identify the ethical dilemma.

2) Why is it an ethical dilemma? Identify the relevant codes.

3) Identify and list information you think would be helpful in making a decision.

4) List at least three possible solutions to this dilemma.

5) Which of the proposed solutions would you choose?

6) Why would you choose this solution?

7) How would you evaluate whether this is a good solution?

Chapter Eight

Service-Learning Requirement Places Psychological Burden on Student

In the sociology department at a large comprehensive university, students who major in sociology can select a track in criminology. One of the required courses in that track is called "Corrections." The course provides a broad overview of the American correctional system, with an emphasis on institutional facilities. For the past two years the professor has incorporated a service-learning component into the course, and students have responded positively. Prior to the introduction of the course's service-learning assignment, the faculty curriculum committee passed a resolution stating that required courses (i.e., those that all students must take to fulfill degree requirements) can include a mandatory service-learning component, as long as this aspect of the course is indicated in the course description in the college catalog.

The "Corrections" course, with the emphasis on the service-learning component, is promoted on the department web site and in the "Sociology Majors' Handbook," an annual publication distributed to all sociology majors. The web site and the handbook include a listing of the types of projects previous students have conducted in the course. Typically, the students develop and implement a therapeutic or educational program for a group of inmates. The professor works with the local prisons before the course begins to determine which group of offenders will be served by the project and outlines the general parameters of the project.

For the current semester, the professor establishes a service-learning project in which the students must develop an exercise program to benefit juvenile sex offenders at the county prison. The prison warden believes that the program will be beneficial to the inmates' rehabilitation.

Kristen is a senior sociology major who is completing the criminal justice track and must complete this course during the current semester in order to graduate with her desired degree. A classmate raped Kristen when she was 16 years old. Kristen successfully brought charges against this individual, who was incarcerated for a short time in a facility in Kristen's hometown that is similar to the service-learning site. After the rape, Kristen underwent therapy, although she is still recovering from the trauma. She has not revealed information about the rape or its aftermath to anyone at college, because she believes that she would be stigmatized if peers knew she had been a rape survivor.

On the first day of class the professor reviews the syllabus and describes the service-learning project to the students. Although Kristen was aware that she would have to do a service-learning project and had reviewed the material describing previous projects, none of the previous projects involved juvenile sex offenders. Thus, she never thought she would be working with this population to complete a course assignment. She is terrified that she will not be able to interact with the inmates in a professional manner or handle the strong emotions she will experience. Just thinking about this project brings back the troubling memories of her own trauma and she becomes visibly distressed. Following class, Kristen anguishes over her possible courses of action. She is extremely reluctant to discuss this matter with her professor, especially since he is male. She is frightened of how he might react and knows that speaking with him about this will be very traumatic for her. Yet she knows if she does not say something, she will have to complete the service-learning requirement. What should Kristen do?

Step 1: Identify and Define the Dilemma

If she does not speak up, Kristen could violate several principles in the student SLC. One of these is to *recognize and reflect upon potential challenges to her personal value system* (SLC I.7). Although Kristen is trying to weigh her alternatives cautiously, failure to discuss these concerns with the faculty member seems to violate SLC I.8, which mandates that students *carefully consider all aspects of the service-learning assignment and consult with faculty members if participation would cause undue distress due to personal circumstances.* If Kristen does not say anything, she will have to participate in the service-learning project. It may be very difficult for her to complete the project in a way consistent with SLC I.3, I.4, I.5, and I.6. If she cannot interact in an appropriate way with the inmates, she will not *adhere to the policies and procedures of the community agency* (SLC I.3), *treat service recipients in a manner consistent with ethical principles* (SLC I.4), and will violate ethical guidelines (SLC I.6). If she avoids interaction with the inmates or in other ways sidesteps her responsibilities with regard to the project, she will not *fulfill her service-learning commitment to the agency in accordance with the course requirements* (SLC I.5).

If Kristen chooses to tell the professor, she will fulfill her responsibility to *carefully consider all aspects of the service-learning assignment* and *consult with faculty members if participation would cause undue distress due to personal circumstances* (SLC I.8). However, the telling itself may cause undue stress, hence the ethical dilemma and the conflict reside in what will cause the greater stress—going through with the project and remaining silent, or having to share her rape with the professor. Even if Kristen does decide to tell the professor, she is not sure how she expects the professor to resolve the problem. If he exempts her from the project, she will not *fulfill her service-learning commitment to the agency in accordance with the course requirements* (SLC I.5). By not doing the project, she will not have the opportunity to *recognize and reflect upon potential challenges to her personal value system* (SLC I.7). How should this dilemma be resolved?

Step 2: Address Relevant Principles and Gather Information

Autonomy and respect for people's rights seems the most relevant principle to apply to this dilemma. According to this principle, Kristen should be allowed to choose her own course of action and thereby have some say in the choice of the service-learning project. This is a laudable solution that would be consistent with the principle of autonomy. However, it would be impractical for a professor of a large class to fully accommodate each student's needs and preferences. The best a professor might do is provide a set of different service-learning projects from which students can choose. The integrity principle requires honesty and the avoidance of deception. Thus Kristen would violate this principle if she chooses not to discuss her reservations with the professor. However, if telling the professor results in Kristen's exemption from the service-learning requirement, then she might not fulfill her course responsibilities, which would be at odds with the fidelity/responsibility principle. This principle also might be put to the test if Kristen attempts but fails to carry out the requirements of the service-learning project in an appropriate manner.

With regard to gathering information, Kristen speaks to her mother and sends an email to her professor requesting more information. She also familiarizes herself with the college policies governing service-learning. Kristen's mother sympathizes with Kristen's dilemma. She asks Kristen whether she should call the professor and speak to him on Kristen's behalf. Kristen's mother feels very strongly that Kristen should not be required to do the service-learning project and asks if there are other college personnel such as the counselor or academic support staff who could intervene on her behalf. Kristen appreciates her mother's willingness to try to take care of the problem for Kristen, but she also feels that it is inappropriate for her mother to do this for her. The response from the professor to Kristen's email essentially reiterates what was on the syllabus and what he said in class. Kristen realizes that the project will involve a significant amount of time interacting with the inmates at the prison. She is now more anxious than ever about participating in the service-learning project. Her perusal of the school's service-learning policy confirms her professor's statement that this project is required for her desired criminal justice track in sociology.

Step 3: Propose Courses of Action

Kristen considers three possible courses of action:

- *Action A:* Say nothing to the professor and complete the service-learning project to the best of her ability.

- *Action B:* Speak to the professor and request an alternative assignment.

- *Action C:* Ask her mother to speak to the professor on her behalf.

Step 4: Determine and Analyze the Consequences for Each Proposed Course of Action

Action A: Say nothing to the professor and complete the service-learning project to the best of her ability.

Positive. By choosing this course of action, Kristen will not subject herself to the stress she knows she will experience if she has to discuss her rape with her professor. Also, this will allow Kristen to continue to abide by her decision not to reveal her rape to anyone. She feels that this decision has helped with her recovery. Further, by forcing herself to do the service-learning project, Kristen can face some of her fears, reflect on the challenges the project will inevitably present for her, and perhaps facilitate recovery from her victimization. Kristen is likely to gain a feeling of confidence and personal strength if she successfully completes the project.

Negative. Although this course of action will avoid the stress of having to reveal her rape to her professor, Kristen may be subjecting herself to even greater stress by participating in the service-learning project. Further, she may find herself reacting to the inmates in a way that is inappropriate. This could cause problems for all involved: herself, the inmates she interacts with, the other students, the warden, and the professor. She may find herself in the position of having to explain her actions to her professor, an explanation that may require telling him about the rape after all.

Action B: Speak to the professor and request an alternative assignment.

Positive. By speaking to the professor, Kristen is recognizing her personal experiences that may interfere with her ability to carry out the service-learning requirements of the course, consistent with the code (SLC I.8). She is empowering herself to acknowledge that she has nothing to be ashamed of. She should expect that the professor will react in a professional and supportive manner, so that there will be no negative repercussions on future interactions as a result of the conversation. By discussing the situation, Kristen and the professor should be able to arrive at a solution that addresses Kristen's concerns and allows her to participate in this service-learning activity or an alternative in order to fulfill course requirements. This conversation and resulting action will be an important learning experience for the professor, who will be more aware of how certain service-learning activities can be problematic for some students.

Negative. By telling the professor about her rape, Kristen is subjecting herself to a great deal of anxiety. Kristen will likely be embarrassed and even ashamed to share this information with him, especially since he is a male professor. Even if Kristen does tell him about the rape and they arrive at an acceptable solution, this may not end Kristen's distress, as she may continue to feel uncomfortable in the professor's presence. She must entertain the possibility that he may view her differently, which may have a negative impact on their relationship. All of these repercussions have a high likelihood of hurting Kristen's academic performance in the class. Finally, the professor may not view Kristen's situation as serious enough to warrant any change in the service-learning requirements. Thus, Kristen will have to do the project in spite of her trauma, so the stress and potentially negative consequences of sharing this information with her professor could be for naught.

Action C: Ask her mother to speak to the professor on her behalf.

Positive. By asking her mother to speak to the professor on her behalf, Kristen is able to avoid the stress of having to reveal the rape directly to her professor. Further, she probably will not have to do the service-learning project, and thus will avoid that distress and any difficulties resulting from inappropriate behavior while conducting the service-learning project. Since there would be no direct conversation between Kristen and her professor, it will be easier to continue to interact with him without feeling embarrassed or ashamed. Her class performance is not as likely to be affected as if she had told the professor directly.

Negative. By having her mother speak on her behalf, Kristen may be viewed by the professor as not acting as a responsible adult. The professor may feel offended that Kristen did not think she could tell him directly. This situation eliminates the possibility for personal growth that might result if Kristen told the professor herself. This course of action also has the same potentially negative consequences of Action B, in that the professor may still treat Kristen differently as a result of knowing about the rape, and she may feel very uncomfortable in his presence. Both of these factors could negatively impact her academic performance. And again, the professor still may decide not to excuse Kristen from the service-learning requirement.

Step 5: Decide on the Best Course of Action

Kristen decides to take Action B: speak to the professor and request an alternative assignment to the service-learning project.

Step 6: Evaluate and Reflect on the Decision

Action B is a difficult step for Kristen to take, but it seems to be the best course of action. Although it will be difficult for her to speak about the rape to her professor, Kristen knows that this will be an important step forward in her own recovery. By finally sharing this crime with someone outside her immediate family, Kristen will be acknowledging to herself that she is blameless and should not feel ashamed that this happened to her. Kristen views this action as a reflection of her ability to act as an adult and to resolve problems herself, even if the required actions are personally challenging.

Kristen and the professor can together decide on the best service-learning project. Then, if they agree that Kristen should attempt to do the project that involves the juvenile offenders, a backup plan can be implemented if that proves too difficult and problems arise—either in terms of Kristen's own well-being or her behavior when interacting with the offenders. Conversely, if Kristen and the professor decide that it would be best to do an alternative service-learning project, they can work out a plan that is mutually acceptable and will be a positive and rewarding experience for Kristen.

Using the pillow test, this decision seems to be the appropriate course of action. Although Kristen will inevitably worry about her conversation with the professor, both before and after its occurrence, she will sleep better than if she said nothing and attempted the service-learning project. The stress of having to work directly with the juvenile offenders and potentially relive the rape in her mind would presumably be much greater and could be very harmful to Kristen's well-being. This would be compounded by her anxiety that she might say or do something that would cause problems. With regard to the newspaper test, Kristen feels that her story of confronting her problems directly would be one she would be proud to read about. Kristen thinks about how her mother and therapist would react to such a story; she decides that they would be very proud of her and view this step as a sign of strength and healing for Kristen. However, the whole situation is certainly not something Kristen would want to see in the paper, so this is not the best test. Finally, with regard to the child test, Kristen believes she will have abided by the maxim, "Honesty is the best policy." She feels that she would be able to explain and justify her decision and actions to a child.

Related Issues

What action should the professor take if Kristen decides to approach him with her concerns? If he exempts Kristen from doing this project, how should that be handled? Other students might wonder why Kristen is not required to do the project. This action may single Kristen out in a way that will make her the focus of the other students' attention. This might create a situation similar to the one that Kristen is trying to avoid. If the professor does not exempt Kristen from the project, he is subjecting her to a situation that might be harmful to her well-being. Moreover, it could be harmful to the other students, the inmates, and the professor's relationship with the community. This action could be viewed as a violation of the faculty SLC, which states that faculty must *minimize potential harm to students* (SLC II.2) and *treat all students in a manner consistent with ethical principles* (SLC II.7).

This situation raises the question of whether faculty can require service-learning without exception. When should exceptions be made in light of students' individual needs and experiences? Which circumstances warrant such exceptions and which do not? As is the case in this hypothetical dilemma, a student in a different situation may be very reluctant to reveal the specifics regarding those circumstances. Is an explanation required if a student approaches a faculty member and states that there has been a stressful event in the student's life that should exempt him or her from the service-learning project? Would a professor's demand for a more complete explanation be an intrusion on a student's privacy?

Additional Dilemma

Rob is an African-American student at a small college that lacks ethnic diversity. He is from a large Midwestern city and grew up in a predominantly African-American neighborhood that is impoverished and crime-ridden. Although Rob never engaged in any significant criminal activity, the police in his neighborhood have targeted him occasionally with minor physical and verbal harassment. Further, Rob witnessed two police officers using excessive, unjustified force on one of his friends. The injuries that resulted from the assault required hospitalization.

In one of Rob's chemistry courses, "The Chemistry of Addiction," students participate in a service-learning project that entails working with teams of students and police officers to present the Drug Abuse Resistance Education (DARE) program at the local high school. Given Rob's past experiences with police, he is extremely reluctant to participate in this project. He firmly believes that he will not be treated with respect by the police because the college town is not ethnically diverse, and he is worried about what the police officers might do while he is present. He is also worried that he might behave in a way that will be viewed as inappropriate by the police. This could get him in trouble and thus have negative repercussions on his class performance. However, he is afraid to bring these concerns to the professor because he is not sure how she will react. What should Rob do?

1) Identify the ethical dilemma.

2) Why is it an ethical dilemma? Identify the relevant codes.

3) Identify and list information you think would be helpful in making a decision.

4) List at least three possible solutions to this dilemma.

5) Which of the proposed solutions would you choose?

6) Why would you choose this solution?

7) How would you evaluate whether this is a good solution?

PART III

Faculty

Chapter Nine

Service-Learning
Code of Ethics for Faculty

Although the recent infusion of service-learning into the curriculum has arisen from multiple sources, faculty have been the front-runners and sustaining force in this movement. The movement's goals are articulated by faculty who firmly believe in service learning and who develop, revise, and assess the curriculum. College curricula have added increasing numbers of service-learning opportunities spanning all disciplines, types of institutions of higher education, and types of community outreach. In parallel with this development, faculty have more fully articulated their own roles and responsibilities as the torch bearers of service-learning pedagogy and as professors committed to helping their students achieve the learning outcomes established for a particular service-learning course.

The faculty section of our service-learning code draws from the rich body of literature that describes best practices in service-learning (e.g., Boss, 1994; Gorman, Duffy, & Heffernan, 1994; Kendall, 1991; Kretchmar, 2001; Valerius & Hamilton, 2001; Zlotkowski, 1998). However, such lists of teaching tips fall short insofar as they are not mandates to which faculty must adhere. Certain responsibilities of the instructor of a service-learning course should be regarded not only as good ideas but also as obligations. That is, if an instructor fully embraces service-learning as a pedagogical method, he or she is bound to provide a learning experience and community benefit consistent with that vision.

Through observance of the guidelines proposed in the second section of the SLC, the implementation of service-learning in a course should be less problematic and more rewarding for the faculty member. More important, these guidelines should help faculty provide the best learning opportunity possible for their students while at the same time meeting their commitment to the community. To the extent that faculty can adhere to this code of conduct, there should be a corresponding decrease in the significant challenges they face when teaching a service-learning course. However, the code will not eliminate all barriers to a successful service-learning experience and will not encompass all situations that may arise. Such cases serve as the basis for the dilemmas proposed in the subsequent chapters in this section.

The faculty section of the SLC is written in chronological order, beginning with the identification of the service-learning project. With institutional support, a faculty member can discover an appropriate service-learning partnership that will achieve the dual aims of service-learning: student learning and civic engagement. Faculty members should ensure when selecting sites that there are no significant physical or psychological risks to the students. This process of matching the site, course objectives, student abilities, and community needs is a complex process that must be executed thoughtfully and carefully. Faculty should use available resources and communicate with involved parties. Some of these resources are discussed in Chapter 20, which examines the topic of risk management in service-learning.

After selecting the site, faculty should work with the community representatives to develop a plan that clearly delineates students' roles and responsibilities at the site, the instructor's expectations for the types of experiences students should have, and the course learning objectives. The expected benefits and outcomes for the agency should also be included.

Having taken these initial steps, the next responsibility of faculty is to develop course materials and assignments that will help students accomplish the learning goals of the course and fulfill the commitment to the agency as set forth in the plan. Students can't be expected to fully realize the faculty member's vision without clearly communicated instructor expectations that include learning and community outcomes, site requirements, assignment guidelines, and pertinent procedures and information (e.g., laws, safety procedures, and contact information).

Students are often unprepared to meet the requirements of service-learning experiences. Although the institution as a whole must play a role, faculty are obligated to provide the necessary training, background information, and personal preparation necessary for the situations and people students are likely to encounter while fulfilling their service-learning responsibilities. This may require soliciting experts to conduct workshops with students, inviting members of the community agency to the class to establish connections and provide critical information, and assigning readings and reflection exercises to demonstrate student preparedness. Consistent with this step is the discussion of ethical dilemmas that may arise in the course of the service-learning experience. This book provides a means by which students and instructors can discuss these dilemmas to increase student preparation for service-learning. This should result in more positive and rewarding outcomes for the faculty member, students, community representatives, and those served.

Having laid a solid groundwork for a successful service-learning project, faculty must remain diligent throughout the project to ensure its continued success. Faculty should regularly allow class time for students to discuss any concerns with regard to their service-learning. Concerns should be discussed individually with the instructor, if desired. Faculty should communicate regularly with the contact person at the service-learning site to assess whether the project is proceeding as planned. We strongly recommend regular visits to the site and whenever possible, direct involvement in the service-learning activities. Faculty who participate in the service-learning activity with students are powerful role models of committed civic engagement and ethical decision-making. Participating faculty are better equipped to deal with unexpected problems. Faculty must be ready and willing to make the necessary adjustments to address these challenges.

Faculty must formally assess the service-learning experience as an obligation to the institution, students, and community agency and as a way to improve their own courses. This assessment can be both formative and summative. For example, the faculty member may want to receive feedback from relevant parties throughout the project to determine if the project is meeting expectations and to determine if the parties understand the process by which the project is being carried out. This endeavor would be formative, in that the faculty member can then use this information to make changes necessary to improve the success of the project. A summative evaluation at the end of the project is also important and should ideally measure both student learning outcomes and benefits to the community. Specific indicators might include performance of course content, a qualitative analysis of reflective journal entries, and client satisfaction surveys. The results of the assessment should be shared with appropriate parties and utilized in future iterations of the course. This topic of service-learning assessment is discussed more fully in Chapter 19.

Although this code will help faculty achieve success in utilizing service-learning in their courses, dilemmas will still arise that cannot be prevented by adherence to this code. Chapter 10 provides several hypothetical dilemmas that exemplify the types of challenges faculty may face when teaching a course that includes a service-learning component.

The following faculty SLC is proposed.

II. Faculty

1) Faculty shall match community needs with academic service-learning goals prior to the beginning of the project to ensure that academic and community service goals can be achieved.

2) Faculty shall minimize potential harm to agencies, their constituents, and students.

3) Faculty shall provide community agencies with a plan that includes information about what is expected and required of students and the agency (e.g., accountability, commitment, consistency, and communication).

4) Faculty shall develop course goals consistent with service-learning objectives and communicate to the students, both verbally and in writing, the parameters of the service-learning requirement, including:

   a) Academic objectives for the service-learning experience

   b) Articulated community benefits

   c) Time requirements

   d) Students' roles and responsibilities

   e) Legal and ethical guidelines on issues such as professionalism, liability, confidentiality, and insurance

   f) Responses to emergencies (e.g., threats, weather, health risks)

   g) Expectations for integration into course material and reflection

   h) Alternative assignment unless college policy requires service-learning

5) Faculty shall properly train and inform students of their responsibilities and potential risks prior to the beginning of the service-learning activity.

6) Faculty shall ensure students understand the diverse characteristics of those with whom they will be working.

7) Faculty shall treat all students in a manner consistent with ethical principles.

8) Faculty shall maintain involvement with community agencies throughout the process and be responsive to changing needs and circumstances.

9) Faculty shall be available to students for consultation or referral for problem solving and conflict resolution.

10) Faculty shall assess the outcomes of this activity for the recipients, the community, and students.

Chapter Ten

Faculty Responsibility
to the Community Agency

D r. Joggar is a professor in a college's social work department. He teaches a course that offers a service-learning component in which the students provide services for a nonprofit community agency. Dr. Joggar and the agency have had a service-learning partnership for the last several years. When Dr. Joggar established initial contact with the agency, he and the agency determined the type of service that would be beneficial to the agency and meet the learning goals for his course. The service consists of identifying clients' needs and providing referrals for those needs. Through their service, the students have a chance to learn about social services available in the area, the needs of the clients, how to listen to the clients, and the referral process. The service-learning experience has gone well for many years, and the students have met the objectives established for the course.

The first step of a student's assignment is to contact Ms. Lambat, the supervisor from the community agency. Dr. Joggar has not, however, regularly restated the goals of the assignments with Ms. Lambat. Thus, he was surprised when the students returned from an early visit to the agency to tell him that the needs of the agency had changed and that Ms. Lambat had given them a new assignment: marketing.

Because it had become more difficult for the agency to find and train community volunteers, the agency management decided to create paid positions. The agency created and financed the positions gradually; in the first year there was one position, in the second two more, and so on. However, the agency had had a drop in the number of clients requesting referral services. In order to retain their current staff, the managers decided that only the paid employees would be responsible for identifying the clients' needs and providing referrals. This was the service that had been partially assigned to Dr. Joggar's students. Since the need was now being fully met by the agency staff, Ms. Lambat no longer needed students to provide the service. However, the agency still needed help in marketing its services to the community.

Since many students continued to do volunteer work at the agency after the course was completed, Ms. Lambat did not remember that Dr. Joggar's requirements for the students were to identify client needs and provide referrals. She believed there would be no problem in shifting the services. However, changing the students' assignment to marketing the agency's services would not provide the students with the learning outcomes Dr. Joggar had originally intended. Most importantly, the agency had provided a training module to prepare students to achieve these outcomes. This training would not be available for the marketing assignment.

Thus, a situation has developed in which the community agency is relying on students to provide a service, but the academic learning objectives for the students are not being met through the experience. What should Dr. Joggar do? Should he continue the service-learning experience, even though the students can't meet the learning objectives of his class?

Step 1: Identify and Define the Dilemma

Dr. Joggar understands that the agency's needs have changed. The agency counts on the marketing services provided by the students in his course. However, to keep the service-learning aspect of the course, Dr. Joggar expects the students to identify clients' needs and provide referrals as indicated in the course objectives. These objectives are no longer being met because Ms. Lambat changed the students' assignment. Without the students' assistance, the referral service will be affected because it needs to be marketed to the community in order to gain clients. The agency is counting on the students to do that job.

Looking at the SLC, Dr. Joggar realizes that even though he has been sensitive about a community need and has tried to help the agency (SLC II.1), he has not provided the agency with the information about what is expected and required of the students on a regular basis (as specified in

SLC II.3). He discussed with Ms. Lambat the agency's needs and the services the students would provide some years ago, at the beginning of the arrangement. Even though he maintains contact with the agency regarding the students' performance, he has not communicated with the agency regarding other issues, and has therefore overlooked the changes in the needs of the agency (SLC II.8).

Should Dr. Joggar change the objectives of his course or the service-learning character of the course? Should he consider a different service at the same agency or contact a different agency that offers the services needed to meet the objectives of the course? What else can he do, since the students have the course syllabus and have already visited the agency and received their assignments?

Step 2: Address Relevant Principles and Gather Information

Dr. Joggar should consider the principles proposed in Chapter 1 and take into consideration the needs of the different parties involved.

The principle of beneficence consists of the act of doing good, that is, determining in whose best interest an action is performed. Dr. Joggar intends to teach the students about social services by providing a service to a community agency. So, with the new assignments, the agency would still benefit from services the students provide. The students would still learn about social services from the marketing assignment, even though they would not meet the course objectives of identifying clients' needs and providing referrals.

The principle of nonmaleficence also applies. Since Dr. Joggar has established a relationship with the agency, Ms. Lambat expects to have students available for the needed services. If the students are not available for the marketing project, the agency may not have enough clients to maintain the referral services. Furthermore, the experience no longer matches the learning objectives for the course. The learning process will be negatively affected if the course's objectives are not met.

Perhaps one more principle will help Dr. Joggar to solve the dilemma. He should determine what his responsibility is to both the agency and to the students in the course. He should determine whether there is a contract with the agency; if the college is involved with the agency in any other way, and what other courses or programs serve the agency.

Dr. Joggar should consult with the community resource person at the college for help in answering these questions. Although Dr. Joggar is in constant contact with Ms. Lambat regarding the students' performance, he should ask himself if he has restated or clarified the goals for the students' assignment often enough. From the students' perspective, Dr. Joggar should consider whether the marketing assignment can be used to meet the course's objectives, and what can be done to relate the two different assignments—identifying clients' needs and referral sources versus marketing—so that the students understand the referral process in an applied fashion.

Step 3: Propose Courses of Action

Based on the type of dilemma and principles applied, Dr. Joggar has several courses of action to consider. He may:

- *Action A:* Change the course objectives.

- *Action B:* Change the service-learning nature of the course.

- *Action C:* Request a change in the assignment given to the students by the agency.

- *Action D:* Keep the new marketing assignment and incorporate the content of the referral training into the marketing training.

- *Action E:* Maintain the initial course objectives by contacting another agency with similar needs.

Step 4: Determine and Analyze the Consequences for Each Proposed Course of Action

Action A: Change the course objectives.

   Positive. A change in objectives would result in a continuation of service for the agency, supplying it with the needed support. The agency would be able to continue marketing the existing service to the community, a strategy that could increase the number of clients.

Negative. By changing the objectives, Dr. Joggar would create a problem for the department regarding the accreditation process. The course objectives are established by an accreditation agency. Changing one course after the courses are established and the objectives are assigned would have an impact on other courses and the curriculum as a whole.

Action B: Change the service-learning nature of the course.

Positive. Allowing the students to keep the marketing project as described by the agency would benefit the agency by providing the support for the marketing needs.

Negative. Even though the students are providing a service, they would not be fulfilling any service-learning requirements. The course would no longer be a service-learning course, because the service is not related to the learning objectives of the course.

Action C: Request a change in the assignment given by the agency to the students.

Positive. The students could benefit from the service-learning experience if Dr. Joggar is able to have the students participate as he initially expected.

Negative. This action may not work, since the agency has the trained staff for the services the students formerly provided, but it still does not have the resources for the marketing component of the services. This action would require referral training for the students and a marketing training for the staff.

Action D: Keep the new marketing assignment and incorporate the content of the referral training into the marketing training.

Positive. This may help the agency as well as the students. Dr. Joggar should ask Ms. Lambat to incorporate the information regarding the available social services into the marketing training. That way, the students can at least partially meet the course objectives. Also, they will have more information regarding the whole referral process, which may enrich the students' presentations to the community and thus attract more clients.

Negative. This strategy may place an added burden on the agency by requiring it to provide additional training that incorporates more information than Ms. Lambat had expected.

Action E: Maintain the initial course objectives by contacting another agency with similar needs.

Positive. A different agency may be able to offer the referral with support from the students. As a result, the students will meet the course's objectives. In following this action, the new agency and the students will benefit.

Negative. The current agency would not be able to market its services to new clients and consequently might not be able to keep the referral service. Since it is a nonprofit agency that depends on funds from different sources and has created permanent positions to serve the clients, the loss of support would have a negative impact on its services and its future. This action might also harm the relationship among the professor, his institution, and the community agency.

Step 5: Decide on the Best Course of Action

Keeping in mind his responsibilities to the agency and the students, Dr. Joggar is ready to determine a course of action from which both parties should benefit. He decides to take Action D, which is a compromise. Since the course has already started and the students already have the assignment from the agency, it is the best option. He has to make sure the students obtain information regarding the social services available in the community, as they had in the original training. Dr. Joggar asks Ms. Lambat to incorporate information from the referral training into the marketing training. That way, the students can provide more comprehensive information to their audience during the marketing campaign, and Dr. Joggar is able, to some extent, to meet the objectives assigned for the service-learning experience.

Dr. Joggar discusses the characteristics of his course's service-learning experience with Ms. Lambat, and they decide that the students can participate in the marketing campaign as long as they are trained on the social services available in the community. Even though the students would no longer participate in the referral services, they still will make contacts with the community. Because they will miss the training in the referral process, however, Dr. Joggar has to make adjustments in the course objectives regarding the service-learning experience.

Step 6: Evaluate and Reflect on the Decision

Dr. Joggar's last step in the decision-making process is to evaluate his decision and its outcomes. He will ask the agency and the students for feedback at the end of the semester. Dr. Joggar and Ms. Lambat's compromise
should lead to positive results. The agency, so far, is satisfied with the outcome of the marketing done by the students. After the first week of presentations, the agency noted an increase in the number of clients looking
for the referral services. In addition, the students are learning not only
about the services available in the community but also the importance of
making those services available.

Dr. Joggar feels he will be able to reach, at least partially, the goal of
the service-learning assignment. He is satisfied with the compromise
reached with the community agency and elated with the enthusiasm
shown by the students. The students appreciate the fact that their services
are really necessary and are having positive results in a short time.

Dr. Joggar applies the pillow, newspaper, and child tests to his decision. He decides that he can sleep with his decision, that he would not
mind seeing his decision on the front page of the newspaper, and that he
would tell a child to follow the same decision, considering the circumstances.

Related Issues

Dr. Joggar's situation exemplifies a breakdown in the communication
process. The lack of communication between the faculty and the community placement agency may cause serious problems. Chapter 20 also highlights the need for planning and communication throughout the whole
service-learning experience.

It is not only important to *match community needs with academic service-learning goals prior to the beginning of the project to ensure that academic
and community service goals can be achieved* (SLC II.1), but also to *provide
community agencies with a plan that includes information about what is
expected and required of students and the agency (e.g., accountability, commitment, consistency, and communication)* (SLC II.3) and to *maintain
involvement with community agencies throughout the process to address
changing needs and circumstances* (SLC II.8).

Additional Dilemma

A class is assigned a service-learning project that consists of planning an event for the community. The community agency director provides guidelines and directions for the project. As the students start working on the project, they obtain information provided by both the community and the agency. The information gathered by the students indicates that their service would not meet a community need. The students discuss the problem with the faculty. They have a dilemma, since the gathered information comes mostly from the agency and indicates that the agency director has not kept up to date with community needs. How should the professor address this dilemma?

1) Identify the ethical dilemma.

2) Why is it an ethical dilemma? Identify the relevant codes.

3) Identify and list information you think would be helpful in making a decision.

4) List at least three possible solutions to this dilemma.

5) Which of the proposed solutions would you choose?

6) Why would you choose this solution?

7) How would you evaluate whether this is a good solution?

Chapter Eleven

Student Poses a Potential Risk in Service-Learning Placement

D r. Heatherton is an associate professor in the economics department of a large private university. One of the courses she teaches, "Economics of Poverty," fulfills a general studies requirement in the social sciences. The course has a service-learning component. The learning goals of the course are for students to understand the governmental and socioeconomic factors that contribute to poverty in the United States and to understand the demographics of those living in poverty. For the service-learning requirement, each student works with an agency to develop and then provide a service designed to benefit a local, economically disadvantaged group. Through this service-learning experience, Dr. Heatherton believes students will gain a more direct and clearer understanding of poverty.

To help students identify an appropriate service-learning site and project, Dr. Heatherton gives the students a list of possible placements and provides examples of what previous students have done to fulfill this course requirement. For the first step, all students write a one- to two-page proposal of the type of service-learning they would be interested in doing and why.

One of the students in the course, Joe, is a second-year business student who is interested in a career as a financial planner. Joe has a privileged and affluent background. He proposes to offer a series of classes on basic financial management (i.e., balancing a checkbook, savings accounts, etc.) to the clients of the local homeless shelter. He also states that he will have one-on-one follow-up sessions with clients to help them apply what they have learned to their own financial situation.

Although Dr. Heatherton thinks this is a good project that fulfills the course requirements, she is concerned about approving the placement because of some statements Joe made in his proposal, as well as a few he has offered in class discussion. It is clear from these comments that Joe has a negative view of the poor. In his proposal he wrote, "I am not sure how much I can really do to help, since it seems that anyone with some intelligence should be able to do these things, but I guess it is worth a try." In class, he stated that those suffering from poverty are to blame for their financial struggles. Further, he said, "My uncle started with nothing and now is a very successful businessman. This is the United States. Anyone can make money if they work hard."

In light of these comments, Dr. Heatherton is deeply troubled by Joe's proposed service-learning experience and sets up a meeting with Joe to discuss these concerns. During the course of the meeting, she expresses her concern that Joe may verbalize his own beliefs in a way that offends the clients. Joe assures her that although he has these beliefs, he will not express them to the clients or employees of the shelter. Joe argues that this experience might open his eyes and perhaps change his views regarding the economically disadvantaged. Dr. Heatherton is inclined to believe Joe is right about that. She has seen many students change from these service-learning experiences. However, the potential for harming the clients is very high. Joe might express his views regarding the origins of poverty to the clients, who would likely react with anger, indignation, and frustration. It could be a humiliating experience for the clients. As a result, the clients might be reluctant to use the services offered by the shelter.

In order to ensure that Joe does not harm the clients in this fashion, Joe will require close supervision by the shelter employees, placing a great demand on already overburdened individuals. It may be that Joe will not be liked or accepted by the shelter employees or volunteers, and thus this placement could create an uncomfortable working environment for all involved. Dr. Heatherton tells Joe she needs to think about his proposal and get back to him. Should she allow Joe to do his proposed service-learning project?

Step 1: Identify and Define the Dilemma

According to the SLC, faculty are obligated to *develop course goals consistent with service-learning objectives* (SLC II.4). Further, SLC II.2 states that faculty shall *minimize potential harm to agencies, their constituents, and students.* This scenario is a service-learning dilemma because these codes are in conflict. If Dr. Heatherton wanted to provide the best learning opportunity for the student, she would approve Joe's placement in the homeless shelter. If the instructor wants to ensure the service-learning project does no harm to the clients, she would deny Joe's request. This potential harm also extends to the shelter employees and volunteers with whom Joe would work. Joe could inadvertently offend one of these workers, as their outlook and beliefs are likely to be very different from his own. He also would place very heavy demands on the employees' and volunteers' time, due to the close supervision Joe would need. Since the workers' time is already at a premium due to inadequate staffing and high caseloads, these time demands may compromise the ability of the employees and volunteers to provide services to persons who come to the shelter seeking help.

SLC II.2 asks faculty to *minimize potential harm to students*. In this situation, again, this code conflicts with SLC II.4: *develop course goals consistent with service-learning objectives*. The service-learning experience could be emotionally trying for Joe. He will probably be exposed to persons and situations he has never experienced. These encounters may challenge Joe's belief system and perhaps some of his core values. Such personal change is often accompanied by much stress and emotional struggle. As a service-learning student, Joe should *recognize challenges to his value system as opportunities for personal growth* (SLC I.7). He may not have the capacity to do this, even if the instructor strives to ensure that he is *properly trained and informed of his responsibilities* (SLC II.5) and *understands the diverse characteristics of those with whom he will be working* (SLC II.6). Further, this personal change could affect his relationship with his family, especially with his mother, who holds views very similar to his own. To resolve this dilemma, Dr. Heatherton must determine which of these codes is most important to uphold, even if there is risk that upholding one may result in violation of another.

Step 2: Address Relevant Principles and Gather Information

The first relevant principle is beneficence. Joe's proposed financial management classes would clearly benefit the members of the shelter. Teaching them how to manage their limited financial resources would facilitate their path to autonomy and self-sustenance. Completing these classes would give them a sense of pride and accomplishment that may lead to a desire for further education. The classes could have a positive impact on the shelter by reducing its clients' reliance on shelter services. This could benefit the community as a whole.

Dr. Heatherton believes Joe would benefit from the experience. Through direct interaction with the shelter clients, Joe will no longer be able to see the clients as a homogeneous group of people who share similar attributes—lack of intelligence, motivation, and initiative. Research has demonstrated that in the proper context such interactions, coupled with reflection exercises that are part of service-learning requirements, are likely to challenge the stereotypes Joe currently holds (Astin, Sax, & Avalos, 1999; Boyle-Baise & Kilbane, 2000; Eyler & Giles, 1999).

The second relevant principle is nonmaleficence. This service-learning placement has the potential to harm all parties involved—the shelter clients, shelter workers, and Joe himself. Joe may either verbally or nonverbally communicate his beliefs to the clients, whether by intention or not. If Joe sends a message that he believes these clients are to blame for their own misfortune, this would be offensive and harmful to the clients. Joe should not judge the clients. Joe's presence may place harmful demands on the shelter workers and create a tense working environment if Joe is not accepted by the employees and volunteers.

Joe could also harm himself. Joe will probably be afraid to be at the shelter and to interact with the clients. This might cause Joe to experience personal turmoil. Is it appropriate for an instructor to place a student in a situation that could cause some psychological distress, even if there are potential benefits? What level of distress is acceptable, and how does an instructor determine that?

The final relevant principle is justice/fairness/equity. Although less prominent than the other two, this principle is relevant with regard to the learning opportunities afforded the students in the class. Is it right to deny Joe this educational opportunity due to his personal beliefs? Many in higher education would argue that to the greatest extent possible, the same learning opportunities must be available to all students. Is it fair to the shelter employees and volunteers, and perhaps more importantly to the shelter clients, for Dr. Heatherton to allow Joe to do this project? Should they be exposed to the potential risk that Joe presents?

Dr. Heatherton decides she needs input from others to help her make the best decision. The first person she consults with is the director of the homeless shelter, whom she knows well. Dr. Heatherton has placed several students at this shelter in the past, all with positive results. She herself occasionally volunteers in the shelter's soup kitchen. Dr. Heatherton explains the situation to the director, paraphrasing components of Joe's proposal. To protect Joe's confidentiality, she does not state his name. She expresses her concerns with regard to the placement. The director replies that he has complete trust in Dr. Heatherton and that he will leave it to her to make the decision. He believes that this experience might be very beneficial to Joe and is willing to provide extra supervision to minimize opportunities for potential harm and maximize learning opportunities for Joe. Dr. Heatherton is reassured, but reluctant to place that kind of burden and responsibility on the director. Would doing so be ethical? It seems that the potential benefit to the shelter, its clients, and Joe might not outweigh that investment and the risks associated with Joe's potentially inappropriate behavior. Such behavior could have a long-term negative impact on the clients. Also, the time the employees and volunteers spend with Joe could be better spent providing services to the clients. Are Joe's potential personal growth and his offer to teach financial management classes worth the risk?

Next, Dr. Heatherton consults with a colleague who also has implemented an extensive amount of service-learning. The colleague says that he would not place Joe in that situation. He believes that it is "just not worth the risk." He asks Dr. Heatherton to consider the threat this poses to the positive relationship she and the academic institution have with the shelter. Damage to this relationship could compromise the opportunity for the homeless shelter to be a service-learning placement for students in the future.

Step 3: Propose Courses of Action

Dr. Heatherton considers four possible courses of action:

- *Action A:* Approve Joe's proposed learning project.

- *Action B:* Approve Joe's proposed learning project with the caveat that Dr. Heatherton will provide additional supervision.

- *Action C:* Deny Joe's proposed learning project and require him to do a term paper alternative.

- *Action D:* Deny Joe's proposed learning project but provide an alternative service-learning experience.

Step 4: Determine and Analyze the Consequences for Each Proposed Course of Action

Action A: Approve Joe's proposed learning project.

   Positive. Joe could experience personal development that results in a much more positive and beneficent view of indigent people. The shelter's clients would probably enjoy and benefit from the financial management classes and personal consulting sessions. The clients might become more confident about their ability to manage their finances and become more aware of opportunities to sustain themselves economically.

   Negative. Joe's views toward the shelter clients and the economically disadvantaged might not change. In fact, the experience could further convince Joe that he is right. Although he is not planning to broadcast his views, a few comments or nonverbal expressions could communicate his negative outlook to the clients. This might anger some of the clients. The shelter workers might also find Joe condescending and aloof. His presence might detract from the sense of support and empathy the employees and volunteers work hard to convey to the clients. The director, although not blaming Dr. Heatherton, might wish he had not been so willing to trust her judgment and to invest his time and energy into Joe. The director might become less open to and more wary of future service-learning placements at the shelter.

Action B: Approve Joe's proposed learning project with the caveat that Dr. Heatherton will provide additional supervision.

   Specifically, Dr. Heatherton will meet with Joe once a week to discuss his interactions with the shelter clients and workers, as well as his reactions to these encounters. She will speak once a week with Joe's supervisor at the shelter to closely monitor Joe's actions at the site.

   Positive. The positive consequences of this action are the same as those in Action A. Also, with the additional supervision by Dr. Heatherton, the learning outcomes for Joe and the potential benefits to the shelter and its clients might be even greater, and less supervision might be needed by the shelter director and the employees.

   Negative. The potential negative consequences of this action are the same as those in Action A, although the additional supervision by Dr. Heatherton should reduce the possibility of those problems. The increased demands on Dr. Heatherton's time to provide additional support to Joe alone could result in new problems for her. Other students may resent the extra time Dr. Heatherton spends with Joe on his service-learning project.

Action C: Deny Joe's proposed learning project and require him to do a term paper alternative.

Positive. The potential harm from this placement would be averted. The clients would not be a potential target of Joe's prejudices. The shelter employees and volunteers would not be burdened by Joe's presence, and the relationship between the shelter and Dr. Heatherton, as well as the academic institution, would be maintained. Joe's term paper could examine the positive impact that financial management classes have had on the economically disadvantaged when they have been conducted in similar venues. Joe might learn through his research that there are additional things that he can do to help the poor.

Negative. The clients would not have the benefit of the classes Joe would have provided. The shelter employees and volunteers would not have the opportunity to share with Joe their alternative view of the economically disadvantaged. The learning outcomes for Joe might be minimal, especially in terms of personal value development. He would probably continue to express the same negative views of the poor.

Action D: Deny Joe's proposed learning project but provide an alternative service-learning experience.

For this alternative, Joe would analyze existing census data to determine unemployment patterns in the county that result from demographic variables. The results would then be provided to the county government, which requested the report.

Positive. This action would have the same positive consequences as in Action C, in that it would avert potential harm to the shelter and its constituents. In addition, the alternative service-learning project could benefit both Joe and the community. By conducting the census data analysis, Joe may find that there are many external causes of poverty. The county could use the information from Joe's report to adjust certain government services to better serve the needy demographic groups Joe identifies.

Negative. This action could have the same negative consequences as in Action C. Specifically, it may not provide the personal growth needed for Joe to change his view of the economically disadvantaged, and the shelter's clients will not reap the benefits of Joe's classes.

Step 5: Decide on the Best Course of Action

Dr. Heatherton decides to take Action D. She denies Joe's proposed learning project but provides an alternative service-learning experience. After further discussion with the shelter director and her colleague, and a review of the service-learning code, she determines that this course of action is the best way to balance the competing codes. The information that Joe gathers could result in beneficial political and social change in the county. Government-funded programs could better target the primary sources of poverty. Also, through this service-learning project, it is likely that Joe will learn that many factors beyond a person's control—such as race, marital status, or gender—can impact his or her socioeconomic status. This awareness could cause him to question his overgeneralization of the causes of poverty and his belief that an individual can always improve his or her financial status with willpower and ability alone. Moreover, Joe will be providing an important service to the community through this alternative placement. The risk of potential harm to the clients and the shelter workers will be eliminated. Other students will not be treated inequitably with regard to Dr. Heatherton's supervision of their service-learning activities.

Step 6: Evaluate and Reflect on the Decision

In order to assess Joe's service-learning project, Dr. Heatherton should examine Joe's journals and have Joe provide a report and give a classroom presentation. The students' journal entries, in keeping with the Dr. Heatherton's guidelines, are reflective pieces that integrate course material and their service-learning experiences. The final journal entry requires that students discuss what they believe they have learned and how their values have changed, if at all, as a result of their project. Dr. Heatherton should obtain feedback from the county agency that receives Joe's report, asking agency officials for their perceptions of the usefulness and probable impact of the report. She should check periodically to see if the report is being used as the county had indicated it would be.

 This course of action still has some drawbacks. Joe may resent not being allowed to carry out his proposal, and his commitment to the alternative project may suffer accordingly. The potential learning outcomes from Joe's service-learning proposal would probably be greater than those

Joe will gain by doing the data analysis and report. The shelter will not have the chance to benefit from the financial planning classes.

When applying the pillow, newspaper, and child tests, Dr. Heatherton is comfortable with her chosen course of action. She will not lose sleep worrying about what Joe might be saying to shelter clients. She imagines that the report findings, if they appeared in the local paper, could galvanize important community efforts to combat poverty. She would be comfortable asking her own child to engage in this opportunity.

Related Issues

One of the underlying issues in this dilemma is Dr. Heatherton's goal for service-learning. She believes that service-learning should result in an increased awareness, understanding, sensitivity, and tolerance for the disadvantaged. She hopes that students who engage in service-learning will develop into more socially responsible and civically committed individuals. Many academic institutions have this goal as part of their academic missions, and service-learning is often touted as one way to reach that goal. Although a goal to develop better citizens through service-learning seems like one that most people would not argue with, it does imply a prescribed set of values that students are expected to acquire. Should an instructor seek to change students' belief systems if they are not consistent with these goals? In the current dilemma, for example, should the instructor's objectives include changing Joe's beliefs concerning the economically disadvantaged? Does an instructor, or an academic institution, have the right, let alone the mandate, to alter students' belief systems? Should that be a component of higher education? How does an instructor assess the development of his or her students' values? If a change in values does not occur, does this mean the student has not fulfilled the learning objectives of the course in which the service-learning is taking place? Or has the instructor in some way failed?

Additional Dilemma

Tara, a biochemistry student, takes a course in which students collect water samples from a lake that is used as a drinking supply for the town in which the university resides. In order to collect these samples, students must wade through a marsh and take boats out to the center of the lake

The project is being supported by a local nonprofit environmental agency whose mission includes ensuring the quality of the lake for both drinking water and to support its wildlife. The instructor plans to have these students collect the water samples each week through the first half of the course and then spend the second half of the course analyzing the samples and preparing a report. The students will present the report at a meeting of the nonprofit environmental group. Tara is physically challenged and uses a wheelchair. Due to her disability, she is not able to enter the water to collect the samples. It also is risky for her to be in the boat, since she cannot swim. How can the professor make accommodations for Tara without compromising the service-learning goals?

1) Identify the ethical dilemma.

2) Why is it an ethical dilemma? Identify the relevant codes.

3) Identify and list information you think would be helpful in making a decision.

4) List at least three possible solutions to this dilemma.

5) Which of the proposed solutions would you choose?

6) Why would you choose this solution?

7) How would you evaluate whether this is a good solution?

Chapter Twelve

Academic Freedom and Service-Learning

Mrs. Harris, a professor in the art department, plans to include a service-learning component in her drawing class in the upcoming semester. She will expect students to engage in three hours of weekly service from 3:00 p.m. to 4:30 p.m. on Tuesdays and Thursdays at one of three local schools, helping elementary school students design and create artwork for their upcoming art fairs.

Mrs. Harris expects her students to keep a record of the days and hours they spend helping these elementary school students. Designated supervisors—either the homeroom teacher or art teacher—will validate the time log. Each student is also to keep a reflection journal for each time period that minimally answers the following questions: What happened today? What did I do? What were the effects of what I did? How does what I am observing and experiencing relate to what we are doing in class?

Mrs. Harris will also ask each student to complete a site evaluation form, and the site supervisor will complete a feedback form. At the end of the semester, students will write a six- to eight-page reflective paper in which they will provide answers to the following questions: What did you learn about these elementary school students and their knowledge of art and art concepts? How did these students benefit from your help? What impact did this experience have on you? How have your ideas about mentoring/tutoring others changed? What did you learn about art and drawing from this experience? What other strategies could be used to improve early learning of art concepts? In what ways could this service-learning activity be improved?

Before the semester begins, Mrs. Harris verbally commits to the principals of three local schools that her students will provide guidance to the fifth- and sixth-grade students on their art projects. She needs to ensure a sufficient number of student participants, so she is hesitant to offer an alternative assignment to this service-learning requirement. In addition, she is having considerable difficulty designing an alternative experience that would incorporate learning through teaching and mentoring, help her students understand younger students' ideas about creating art projects and art concepts, and satisfy a community need. Reluctantly, she considers two ideas for those students who are unable to participate in the service-learning experience at an elementary school. One alternative assignment would involve tutoring classmates. The other would be to write a research paper. Neither option fully satisfies the criteria Mrs. Harris has established. She is concerned not only about achieving the learning outcomes but also about fulfilling her obligations to the elementary schools and their students.

Step 1: Identify and Define the Dilemma

This scenario portrays a dilemma caused by conflict among several sections in the service-learning code. Mrs. Harris has already made a commitment to the schools to have her students mentor elementary school students for three hours per week. She has two concerns. First, some of her students might not be able to engage in this activity because of scheduling conflicts. Second, if she offers an alternative assignment, several students in addition to those who genuinely have a scheduling conflict might not participate in the after-school program. In this case, two codes of ethics are in conflict (SLC II.1 and SLC II.4h). Mrs. Harris has matched community needs with her academic service-learning goals, but may be unable to ensure that these goals are achieved.

Her university does not have a policy related to service-learning and therefore administration feels she must offer an alternative assignment. This is in accordance with the service-learning code, which says that if a college or university does not provide clear, written guidelines for service-learning, then faculty need to offer an alternative assignment (SLC II.4h). Faculty create learning experiences in the classroom to empower students, develop their sense of pride, and help them make connections between themselves and the larger community. Faculty use syllabi to target these goals, and they anticipate that students will use the syllabus as a guide to understanding course objectives and requirements. Students understand that, through the syllabus, a professor conveys his or her expectations and goals for that class (SLC II.4). As a result, offering alternative assignments may lead to an inability to meet the objectives stated in the syllabus.

Mrs. Harris remains torn between her obligations to the service sites, her academic freedom to determine the best strategies for understanding course material, and university policy. To resolve this dilemma, she considers several ethical principles and consults with a colleague.

Step 2: Address Relevant Principles and Gather Information

Several principles apply to this dilemma. Because Mrs. Harris arranged with the elementary school principals to provide guidance and mentoring to their students, she has a responsibility to fulfill this commitment. She also has a responsibility to her own students. From her perspective, this activity will provide an educational benefit to all her students, and she questions the need to offer an alternative assignment.

Other ethical principles apply. Beneficence involves providing a benefit to others. Mrs. Harris regards this activity as worthwhile for all involved. In addition, she sees the need to respect her students' rights but recognizes that respect for people's rights includes all parties in the relationship.

At this point, Mrs. Harris consults with a colleague. He agrees that the service-learning component could be a useful way for her students to learn more about project development and creative drawing, and he encourages her to remain committed to her goals for the course. He warns her that her chair and other members of the department are uninformed about the pedagogic value of service-learning and may not support her teaching strategy. Although Mrs. Harris believes that the best interests of the students, the community, and the university would be served, she is concerned about the commitment she has made to the schools and her position in the department. Yet she has exercised her academic freedom by developing and outlining what she believes is an effective pedagogical strategy to achieve course goals.

Step 3: Propose Courses of Action

According to the ethical decision-making model, the next step involves the identification of various courses of action. Mrs. Harris will consider the consequences of each action and determine the best course to follow. She considers three possible actions:

- *Action A:* Require all students to participate in the service-learning activity.

- *Action B:* Offer an alternative activity.

- *Action C:* Contact the three elementary schools and withdraw her commitment to provide student art-fair mentors.

Step 4: Determine and Analyze the Consequences for Each Proposed Course of Action

Action A: Require all students to participate in the service-learning activity.

Positive. This action provides that Mrs. Harris remain committed to her original course guidelines and require all students to participate in 30 hours of service-learning during the semester. From her years of experience teaching drawing, Mrs. Harris believes that service-learning is an effective pedagogical strategy for this class, and therefore feels this requirement is not unreasonable. Mrs. Harris's students would learn more about art by instructing and assisting other students. They would also achieve a sense of accomplishment and self-satisfaction through these mentoring activities. And, the elementary school students would have the opportunity to interact with older students and receive creative assistance with their projects.

Negative. Mrs. Harris recognizes that some students could have other classes or work commitments between 3:00 p.m. and 4:30 p.m. Some students would probably be able to change their work schedules, but not their class schedules. She is also concerned that some students might resent being required to interact with elementary school students. If not committed, her students could provide inadequate guidance and be poor role models. In addition, Mrs. Harris is worried that if she requires service-learning of all her students, it could jeopardize her position at the university because of poor student evaluations.

Action B: Offer an alternative activity.

Positive. Mrs. Harris could offer an alternative assignment such as a research report or the opportunity to tutor classmates. Because students would be able to choose to mentor elementary students, tutor fellow students, or complete a research report, they would be more committed to their choice. This alternative would eliminate students' scheduling conflicts.

Negative. Mrs. Harris believes that the quality of out-of-class and in-class experiences will be different for those who do not engage in service-learning. The alternative option will be offered to the entire class, and if several students select this option, it could compromise classroom learning experiences as well as Mrs. Harris's commitment to the elementary school principals. A research report may not be a comparable experience, and tutoring peers may not be a viable option if no students in her class want to be tutored.

Action C: Contact the three elementary schools and withdraw her commitment to provide student art fair mentors.

Positive. This would be a relatively easy option for Mrs. Harris. She could simply call the three principals and explain that scheduling and other complications prevent her from including this requirement this semester.

Negative. Mrs. Harris has a personal and an institutional obligation to fulfill this commitment. She is concerned that by withdrawing her commitment, her credibility and the college's reputation in the community would be adversely affected and future service-learning opportunities might be unavailable.

Step 5: Decide on the Best Course of Action

Despite her arrangements with these schools, Mrs. Harris is concerned about her student evaluations and those students who would not be able to participate. She selects Action B and offers two alternatives to the service-learning activity. She remains committed to student public engagement, response to community needs, and good citizenship, but recognizes that this can create a professional and personal ethical dilemma.

Step 6: Evaluate and Reflect on the Decision

Although students would be pleased to have a choice of activities and would probably give Mrs. Harris's teaching a favorable evaluation, she might find that class discussion will falter during the semester. If, for example, 15 students engage in service-learning, and 14 students choose the research paper assignment, it could be difficult to create classroom activities related to service-learning experiences that effectively engage all 29 students.

Mrs. Harris understands that it is unrealistic to expect all students to participate in the service-learning project, but she is concerned about her ability to create classroom activities for small-group discussion and reflection on these experiences. She considers recruiting additional service-learning sites in the future so that a range of times could be offered to students. She concludes that the alternative assignments she offers may not be useful and decides to brainstorm more effective substitutes for future classes. Because of her desire to remain connected to the education professionals and art teachers at the local schools, Mrs. Harris is unwilling to withdraw her support. She feels that sending fewer students than planned is better than canceling the project completely.

Applying the pillow, newspaper, and child tests, Mrs. Harris believes that she can sleep with this decision. She would be comfortable with having her decision published in the school newspaper and with explaining her decision to a child. She believes that although the development of this service-learning activity did not unfold as planned, the benefits will outweigh the difficulties she encountered. She feels that those students who participate in the service-learning experience will report a rich and profitable learning experience that will enhance class discussions and their understanding of art and art concepts.

Related Issues

This dilemma raises several related issues. Mrs. Harris is concerned that her academic freedom and her professional integrity and credibility may be compromised. Her desire to provide an effective and creative method of teaching is at odds with her goal of maintaining her position at the university. She is torn between institutional guidelines and fidelity to her beliefs about teaching and nurturing students.

Student evaluations are an integral part of any faculty member's position in a university. If a professor's course goals are not supported by administration, students may question the professor's credibility. This, in turn, can affect student evaluations of that faculty member. Mrs. Harris's ethical dilemma is pertinent to the part of the service-learning code that relates to administrators (see Chapter 14).

Additional Dilemma

Mr. Ryan, a chemistry professor, submits a proposal to the chair of his department to incorporate a service-learning component into an advanced chemistry course. Mr. Ryan proposes 25 hours of chemistry work with middle and high school students. On the first day of class, he plans to hand out clearance forms, an explanation of the process, and a preliminary list of five after-school programs. In all locations, a mentor will be provided by the sponsoring school. According to Mr. Ryan, the 25 hours can be in class or as a tutor. Each student will be expected to keep a journal and share service-learning experiences with the class in a brief oral presentation. A three- to five-page paper also will be required. The service-learning component will be worth 20% of the overall grade.

The chair of the chemistry department is unsupportive and negative. He is concerned only with covering the topics in the syllabus. He believes that service-learning participation should be optional, and that it would be unfair to give points for service-learning projects that might result in a higher grade for those students who participate. Finally, he does not think service-learning activities are a good fit with chemistry courses. What should Mr. Ryan do?

1) Identify the ethical dilemma.

2) Why is it an ethical dilemma? Identify the relevant codes.

3) Identify and list information you think would be helpful in making a decision.

4) List at least three possible solutions to this dilemma.

5) Which of the proposed solutions would you choose?

6) Why would you choose this solution?

7) How would you evaluate whether this is a good solution?

Chapter Thirteen

Misuse of Results of Service-Learning Research Project

D r. Akari is an assistant professor in the education department of a midsize public university. This university is one of the primary feeder institutions for elementary and secondary education teachers to the region's public schools. As one of the electives for the education major, Dr. Akari teaches a special topics course that includes a service-learning component. This course is open to all students seeking certification in secondary education.

Although Dr. Akari knows that students learn extensively from observation and the practicum requirements of the teacher certification program, he also believes students should engage in a service-learning project designed to benefit high school students. Dr. Akari believes that this experience provides a unique and valuable learning opportunity for the teachers-in-training. Projects like these have enabled college students to interact with high school students on a more equal and informal basis. Previous students have indicated in their journals that this interaction has resulted in a better understanding of the concerns and challenges that high school students face, not only in terms of academics but also with social and personal issues.

Dr. Akari first arranges a meeting between the members of his class, student representatives from the local high school, and several teacher liaisons who are willing to assist with the project. Based on this meeting, the class proposes and plans a service-learning project that addresses a need or area of concern for the high school students. The college students decide to assess a tutoring program that is offered in the high school by a local nonprofit agency. The school board has authorized the high school to pay the agency a fee to provide the program. The organization's mission is to improve educational outcomes for at-risk high school students. The agency is offering this program for the second time in the upcoming term. Based on conversations with the high school students and teachers involved with the program, the college students got a sense that some believe this program is highly effective. Students and teachers evaluate the program positively because the students enjoy working with the tutors. The teachers believe that the tutors serve as positive role models for the high school students. Thus, in addition to its potential for helping with schoolwork, the tutoring program affords the students an opportunity for positive social interactions. However, other students and teachers are skeptical about the program. Through systematic evaluation of the program, the students hope to provide empirical evidence regarding the program's impact and identify potential ways to improve it.

Working with Dr. Akari and representatives of the nonprofit agency that sponsors the tutoring program, the university students finalize their plan to assess the program's effectiveness. They develop a questionnaire that measures affective reactions to the program and teachers' perceptions of the impact of the program on its participants. In addition, the students obtain permission from the school and parents of participants to assess academic performance before and after the program. With the aid of a few high school teachers and the program facilitators, the university students administer this questionnaire to the program participants. They also collect relevant data from the school's academic records database. Next, the students analyze the data with Dr. Akari's assistance.

The results of the analysis yield mixed results, confirming the contradictory comments that were heard from the high school students and teachers. Specifically, the students and teachers rated the program very highly and perceived the program as having a positive impact on academic performance. However, the actual academic grades of the high school students who participated in the program did not significantly improve in the subsequent term. Based on these results, the university students write a report to the high school principal that summarizes their findings and makes a few recommendations that they believe would improve the program's effectiveness in terms of actual academic performance.

A few weeks after the report's submission, Dr. Akari receives a letter from the principal thanking Dr. Akari and the students for their work. The principal asks Dr. Akari to present the class findings to the school board. The principal writes that she plans to request additional funding from the board to expand the program so that the number of student participants can be increased. In the letter to Dr. Akari, the principal acknowledges that the results of the analysis are not wholly supportive of the effectiveness of the program, but says she hopes Dr. Akari would be willing to make his presentation more positive and supportive of the program. The principal states that she will carefully scrutinize the results and will seriously consider implementing the recommendations made in the report. However, she asks if Dr. Akari would not mention the equivocal findings so that the program funding will be maintained and possibly expanded.

Although she acknowledges the need for improvement in the program, the principal clearly believes that it is extremely important for Dr. Akari not to give the school board any reason to question whether the board should continue financial support for the program. In the principal's view, the results that did not demonstrate a positive impact on actual academic performance can be worked on, but it is imperative that a united, positive front be presented to the board to avoid jeopardizing the program's existence.

Dr. Akari is deeply troubled by this request. The program did have some positive results, in terms of participants' perceptions and satisfaction with it, so there is some evidence to support its continuation. However, the results indicate that the impact could be strictly affective, which does not meet the program's primary goal of improving actual academic performance. Is it appropriate for Dr. Akari to misrepresent the findings to help solicit continued funding? Should Dr. Akari agree to do the presentation?

Step 1: Identify and Define the Dilemma

According to the SLC, faculty are obligated to *maintain involvement with community agencies throughout the process and be responsive to changing needs and circumstances* (SLC II.8). Further, SLC II.10 states that faculty must *assess the outcomes of this activity for the recipients, the community, and students.* If Dr. Akari wishes to be responsive to community needs, as the SLC indicates, then he should seriously consider conceding to the principal's request. By giving the presentation that the principal requested, Dr. Akari would help fulfill the high school students' needs, which, according to the principal, would benefit greatly from this program. By presenting the program in its most positive light, Dr. Akari would help maintain financial support for the program and thus would be responding to the needs of the agency (SLC II.8). However, by doing so, Dr. Akari would not be accurately presenting the outcomes of the assessment of the activity (SLC II.10). These two codes conflict, creating a service-learning dilemma.

Step 2: Address Relevant Principles and Gather Information

The first relevant principle is beneficence. The program presumably improves student attitudes toward academics and teachers' views of these students. This seems to be a positive outcome that could benefit all.

The justice/fairness/equity principle is also relevant. Is justice served by skewing the results of this assessment for the greater good of maintaining the funding of the program? One could argue that such an effort is highly unjust; it is not fair to the public supporters of the university to continue to provide financial support to a losing proposition.

Finally, and perhaps most central, is the principle of integrity. By doing as the principal asks, Dr. Akari may be violating this principle. By engaging in this behavior, does Dr. Akari violate his own moral code, and act in a way that reflects negatively on his profession and the university?

With regard to gathering information, Dr. Akari decides he must first get input from his students regarding how to proceed. He feels this is important for two reasons. First, he feels that the students are the primary owners of the project and should have some say in how the results are used. Second, he recognizes the potential learning opportunity for the students. Although the class is over, he makes every effort to contact the students and explain the ethical dilemma he is facing. Unfortunately, he only hears from a few students, whose responses are mixed. A few students believe that it would do no real harm to give the presentation the principal is requesting, and that the potential benefit far exceeds any cost associated with that endeavor. Other students believe that it would be highly unethical to present only the positive results of the study. These students believe that Dr. Akari should deny the principal's request.

Dr. Akari emails a colleague at another institution who has been heavily engaged in community-based research. He hopes that she can help, given her extensive experience with this type of work. The friend's response is that if she were faced with this situation, she would give the presentation on the condition that Dr. Akari be allowed to continue to work with the high school in order to evaluate the impact of recommended changes on the program. She says that she would take this action because she would need continued access to the high school to continue her research projects. Dr. Akari understands the value of this view, although he recognizes that it is from the perspective of a researcher rather than an educator.

Step 3: Propose Courses of Action

Dr. Akari considers four possible courses of action:

- *Action A:* Agree to the principal's request that Dr. Akari present only the positive findings to the school board.

- *Action B:* Agree to the principal's request, but only if the principal will allow Dr. Akari to present the negative results as well.

- *Action C:* Deny the principal's request.

- *Action D:* Deny the principal's request, but tell the principal that she may present the findings at the school board meeting as she sees fit.

Step 4: Determine and Analyze the Consequences for Each Proposed Course of Action

Action A: Agree to the principal's request that Dr. Akari present only the positive findings to the school board.

Positive. By giving the presentation the principal has requested, Dr. Akari would help the school maintain a program that the student and faculty participants evaluated favorably, at least in some aspects. For students at risk of dropping out of school, positive regard for a school program is not a trivial finding. The principal has assured Dr. Akari that she will seriously consider the implications of the negative results with regard to academic performance and will strive to implement some of the students' recommendations with regard to these findings. Dr. Akari will be able to maintain positive relations with the high school, which will help ensure continuation of this service-learning opportunity for future students. If the presentation helps achieve continued and expanded funding for the program, the agency can revise the program to increase its efficacy in improving academic performance. Continued evaluation of the program would be an excellent future service-learning project for Dr. Akari's course.

Negative. By agreeing to the principal's request, Dr. Akari has agreed to present misleading results to the school board. This may be viewed as a violation of the professional ethics to which Dr. Akari is bound by his profession. Dr. Akari would not want his students to falsely present their research findings; can he hold himself to a lesser standard? Do the ends justify the means? An astute board member might ask about the program's impact on actual student performance. What would Dr. Akari say? Also, even if the recommendations of the students are implemented, there is no guarantee that this change will lead to the program being effective in improving academic performance. Dr. Akari may be advocating the use of precious school and nonprofit monies to support an ineffective program. The school has many needs and the money might be better spent where it might have a more useful impact.

Action B: Agree to the principal's request, but only if the principal will allow Dr. Akari to present the negative results as well.

Positive. If the principal will agree, Dr. Akari can give the presentation as requested, and thus show his support for the school and maintain his positive relationship with the school. By giving a presentation that accurately represents the actual findings, Dr. Akari would not compromise his professional ethical standards.

Negative. The principal might not agree to this request, and thus the opportunity to discuss the students' findings with the board would be lost. The principal might then feel free to present the results as she chooses, which could be even more misleading than the presentation Dr. Akari would have given if he had agreed to the original request. Dr. Akari would lose control over the use of the results, although that could occur regardless of the course of action he chooses. If the principal does agree to the request, Dr. Akari's presentation, including the negative findings, might result in the reduction or elimination of funding for the program. Would Dr. Akari be comfortable with that outcome? He is in full agreement with his students that there is some value in the program and does not feel that the program should be eliminated entirely. The program could be very effective if the recommended improvements are implemented.

Action C: Deny the principal's request.

Positive. By refusing to present the students' results in a misleading manner, Dr. Akari would uphold his professional and ethical standards. He would honor the students' hard work by not playing a role in the misuse of these findings to serve the principal's agenda. This action would send a clear message to the principal, which might lead her to reconsider her initial request.

Negative. Dr. Akari would forego the opportunity to present the students' findings to the board. The alternative presentation that the principal might give may not reflect the actual results. Dr. Akari must consider how the students would feel about this misrepresentation of their work. Further, a blatant denial of the principal's request would surely displease her. This tension might damage the positive relationship Dr. Akari currently enjoys with the principal, potentially jeopardizing future service-learning opportunities at the school. It could also damage the university-public school collaborative efforts, such as student teaching placements. Such an effect would seriously harm the education program and potentially the university as a whole.

Action D: Deny the principal's request, but tell the principal that she may present the findings at the school board meeting as she sees fit.

Positive. This choice would have many of the same benefits as in Actions B and C. By washing his hands of the matter, Dr. Akari recognizes that the principal can act as she believes she should. If it is not an action he agrees with, Dr. Akari is free to remove himself from the situation completely. He can feel comfortable that he would not jeopardize the program's funding by presenting the negative results.

Negative. One could argue that this option is the easy way out and, through inaction, Dr. Akari would be encouraging the principal to present the students' findings in an inaccurate manner. By telling the principal she should do as she thinks best, Dr. Akari would in effect be saying that although he will not do the presentation himself, it would be acceptable to him if she does. The students and others might view this as a failure to adhere to the ethical principles involved.

Step 5: Decide on the Best Course of Action

Dr. Akari decides to take Action B: Agree to the principal's request, but only if the principal will allow him to present the negative results as well.

Step 6: Evaluate and Reflect on the Decision

Action B seems to be the best course of action. The risk of this choice is that the funding of the entire program could be jeopardized. Yet to Dr. Akari, this seems an acceptable risk, as he can not accept the choice to misrepresent the students' work, either explicitly or implicitly. By presenting the results himself, Dr. Akari can state the tutoring program's insignificant impact on academic performance, argue strongly for the importance of the findings that the student participants and the teachers like the program, and explain why those findings alone might be sufficient justification for continuing and expanding the program. This action would be better than having to hedge a question for which Dr. Akari is unprepared (a likely event if he chose Action A), or allowing the principal to present the results (Action C), as Dr. Akari can speak to the results with greater expertise.

Does this decision pass the pillow, newspaper, and child tests? Dr. Akari knows that if he chose to misrepresent the results of the analysis, himself or by allowing the principal to do so, he would not be able to sleep well. He feels that doing so would be unethical, akin to lying, and would plainly violate the principle of integrity. Dr. Akari imagines a scenario in which a reporter discovered that the presentation was misleading and published that discovery in the local newspaper. The damage to him, the students, the high school, and the university would be significant. The potential loss of the program due to the results would not be a positive news story either, but it would be a better alternative. In the best case, Dr. Akari imagines a story that speaks to his students' hard work, the positive aspects of the program, and the school board's decision to continue the funding provided that efforts are made to improve the program. Finally, Dr. Akari believes Action B best balances the competing codes and his own ethical principles. He is confident that he could justify his choice of action to a child and to the students themselves.

Related Issues

This dilemma raises the question of who owns the products of service-learning. In this case, the students' outcomes consisted of a set of data. Service-learning activities yield a wide variety of outcomes: data, educational programs, marketing materials, information databases (potentially containing sensitive material), statistics about treated clients, and more. These products exist due to the collaborative efforts of the students, instructors, and service-learning site agents. If any of these parties wishes to access and use these products, they should be allowed to do so, given their partial ownership. However, what if their planned use of these products is not viewed as acceptable by one of the other vested parties? Do students or their instructors have the right to say how the agency may use the products of the students' labors? Can an instructor demand access to a data set for educational or research purposes that the instructor's class created on behalf of an agency? If such conflicts arise, there is a question of how they should be resolved, and by whom. Ideally, these issues should be discussed and worked out prior to the onset of the service-learning, as part of the original agreement between the agency and the instructor. There should also be a mechanism in place for conflict resolution, if the agreement does not fully cover the situation.

Additional Dilemma

A professor who is heavily involved in service-learning assesses the extent to which his students' service-learning experiences are helping achieve the stated objectives: increased interest in civic engagement, increased cultural sensitivity, and improved critical thinking skills. The results of his assessment show no significant impact of service-learning on these goals. The professor, although concerned by these results, believes there were several methodological limitations that likely played a crucial role in the lack of significant findings. The professor mentions these findings to the provost. He tells the provost he is planning a follow-up study that should do a better job of addressing the question of the impact of service-learning on the learning objectives.

Despite this cautionary statement, the provost asks the professor to write a report based on these assessment results. The institution is facing severe budget cutbacks due to a sluggish economy. The provost wants to send the report to the board of trustees to support the provost's decision to severely cut funding of the university's service-learning center, including the funding to a staff person. How should the professor respond to the provost's request?

1) Identify the ethical dilemma.

2) Why is it an ethical dilemma? Identify the relevant codes.

3) Identify and list information you think would be helpful in making a decision.

4) List at least three possible solutions to this dilemma.

5) Which of the proposed solutions would you choose?

6) Why would you choose this solution?

7) How would you evaluate whether this is a good solution?

PART IV

Administrators

Chapter Fourteen

Service-Learning
Code of Ethics for Administrators

As discussed in the preface of this book, institutions of higher learning have historically developed in response to community and student needs. These needs are often reflected in the mission, vision, and goals of colleges and universities. Some of these goals are to facilitate student examination of personal value systems, to encourage students to consider the value systems of others, and to make a difference in the lives of members of the larger community. In an opinion poll conducted by the *Chronicle of Higher Education* (Fish, 2003), 65% of the respondents indicated that the most important goal for higher education is to "prepare students to be responsible citizens" (p. 5). Part of this mandate is being accomplished through university support of service-learning activities. Academically based and socially relevant activities in the community not only enhance student self-esteem and sense of pride but also provide societal benefits (Astin, Vogelgesang, Ikeda, & Yee, 2000; Osborne, Hammerich, & Hensley, 1998; Strage, 2000).

It is essential to empower students to contribute to the community and to support service-learning as a legitimate academic enterprise. However, it is not enough simply to recognize service-learning best practices and benefits for students and community partners such as reduction of prejudice, resolution of real-world problems, satisfaction of community needs, recognition of sociocultural differences, and values clarification. College administrators and staff also need to provide a long-term commitment and willingness to work with local community representatives for their benefit. This should be a primary goal, not one that is secondary to the institution's stature. This requires that the community, not the college or university, define its needs and issues. The college or university may have competing interests, values, politics, and economics. However, once the college or university makes a commitment to the community, the integrity of the institution can be jeopardized by a failure to support and maintain its relationship with the community. There needs to be a clear understanding of the college's responsibilities to the community, an acceptance of the educational reasons for being involved with the community, and recognition of the value that these projects bring to the community.

In addition to playing an active, sustained, and beneficial role in the larger community, colleges and universities have a moral obligation to their students to provide opportunities for them to develop into independent, productive, and critical thinkers. In this regard, college administrators can model community engagement, institutionalize acceptance and support for service-learning, and encourage students to become participatory citizens.

The development of role modeling and mentoring skills is part of any useful college activity. These activities include teachers mentoring their students, students mentoring and tutoring in the community, and students mentoring their peers. Service-learning offers an opportunity for students to explore, experiment, and develop interests in mentoring, tutoring, and civic engagement. In addition, experiential learning enhances potential leadership behaviors. Leadership requires vision, imagination, passion, and courage. A leader is someone who helps others grow and develop by teaching them skills and serving as a mentor. All these qualities can, at least partially, be developed through service-learning activities. Student service-learning experiences can provide opportunities for vision clarification, creativity, individuality, goal setting, problem solving, and team building. All of these are useful leadership skills. Therefore, service-learning not only affords students opportunities to question and explore their place in society, but also to practice effective leadership behavior.

Once an institution's vision has been defined, goals established, and a plan implemented to achieve these goals, the institution needs to determine whether its goals fit into the larger cultural context of the college or university system. In order to realize this vision, administrators need to provide support services for faculty, reward systems that encourage faculty participation, and tools for program assessment. Service-learning is a labor-intensive activity that should not be a risky undertaking for faculty.

Therefore, in a receptive campus culture, recognition of the extra effort and logistics involves support for tenure and/or promotion, professional development opportunities, workshops to educate faculty on course integration and assessment, and opportunities for mentoring peers in the implementation of service-learning projects.

Campus barriers to service-learning include resource limitations, poor community relations, and lack of student involvement in the educational process. These barriers can be overcome by providing a centralized and formal administrative center on campus for service-learning activities along with a tradition of service, institutional advocacy, support for faculty, and a voice in the community. Academically based service-learning centers are more successful than centers that are part of the student affairs office.

With this in mind, the SLC proposes that college and university administrators support service-learning projects, institutionalize civic engagement, provide faculty and students with guidelines on liability and ethical issues, and offer faculty opportunities for training and education in service-learning curriculum infusion.

Before providing a few ethical dilemmas that relate to the responsibilities of administrators in the service-learning process, we repeat that part of the SLC below.

III. Administrators

1) Administrators shall recognize and support opportunities for service-learning as part of a liberal education.

2) Administrators shall provide mechanisms for the institutionalization of civic engagement, and resources for service-learning participation and service-related research.

3) Administrators shall be sensitive to and knowledgeable about community needs.

4) Administrators shall make every effort to minimize risky and unsafe locations and circumstances.

5) Administrators shall provide clear guidelines to faculty and students regarding liability and ethical issues.

6) Administrators shall provide faculty with opportunities for training and education in service-learning curriculum infusion.

7) Administrators shall treat all constituents in a manner consistent with ethical principles.

Chapter Fifteen

University Policies and Faculty Implementation of Service-Learning

The following dilemma provides an example of the kinds of impediments faculty face as they attempt to engage their students in service-learning projects. In this case, administrators have been unwilling to provide a special designation for service-learning courses, and this has created some confusion and frustration among students. Many students register for a class without knowing that part of the course requirement is to spend additional time out of class volunteering at a local community agency.

Each semester, Dr. Hursh teaches a professional/technical writing class to upper-class students. His goals for this class are for students to learn skills in editing, creative and original writing, and attentive and appreciative reading, and to participate in 25 hours of service-learning. He wants students to learn about reading and writing through hands-on experiences in the larger community. Dr. Hursh has made arrangements with a local nonprofit agency that provides vocational training, assessment services, job placement, adult development training, and personal work adjustment training to clients with mental retardation and physical disabilities. Dr. Hursh's students are to offer their writing services to this agency during the semester. As service learners, he expects students to keep a weekly learning log that reflects on the quality of their service experience. At the end of the semester, students are to submit a portfolio of writing that they have completed for the agency.

Several of Dr. Hursh's students believe that because the university did not identify this as a service-learning course, they are not prepared and will be unable to complete course requirements. These students state that it is impossible to structure their academic and personal responsibilities when critical information regarding course requirements is missing. Dr. Hursh understands their concerns, but is unwilling to change his syllabus and the requirements for the class. The students follow protocol by first talking to the chair of the English department. He refers them to the dean of liberal arts and sciences, who refers them to the vice president of academic affairs. In the end, students expect the vice president to resolve this issue for them.

Step 1: Identify and Define the Dilemma

The university's mission is to treat students with dignity and fairness as it provides a liberal education that includes an understanding of community needs and contribution to the larger community. These tenets are covered in SLC III.1 and SLC III.7, which state that *administrators shall recognize and support opportunities for service learning* and *treat all constituents in a manner consistent with ethical principles.* At the same time, students must be given ample support and opportunity to complete all course requirements: *Administrators shall provide mechanisms for the institutionalization of civic engagement and resources for service-learning participation and service-related research* (SLC III.2).

Step 2: Address Relevant Principles and Gather Information

The principles of beneficence, fidelity, and responsibility apply as colleges and universities work to promote an enhanced quality of life among students and the larger community. Supported by the institution's social mission and strategic plans, administrators need to articulate and inspire a financial, moral, and resource commitment to public engagement and social responsibility. Within this framework, there needs to be sustained dialogue among the foundation and trustee board members, faculty, students, staff, and community partners. This is in addition to the need for curricular support. The common interests and goals of the larger community and the university can provide the foundation for blending service and learning goals.

In this particular dilemma, because the vice president is unclear about the university's position on curricular content, he contacts the teachers' union, other administrators, the department chair, and the college dean. The union leadership and Dr. Hursh's department chair support and encourage Dr. Hursh's efforts to infuse academically based community service into his professional writing course. However, the dean of liberal arts and sciences is relatively unfamiliar with this pedagogical strategy and unsure about its utility. Therefore, the dean counsels the vice president to encourage Dr. Hursh to use traditional teaching methods.

Step 3: Propose Courses of Action

Institutions of higher learning are expected to be student centered. They are responsible for providing an enriched educational environment that promotes reasoning and critical thinking skills, civic and individual responsibility, personal and professional ethical behavior, and educational training. The ethical principles of beneficence, fidelity, and responsibility are focal issues as educators influence future workers and citizens.

Because Dr. Hursh's students have asked several administrators to resolve an issue, the next step in the decision-making process is to identify various courses of action. The vice president of academic affairs has been designated to address this issue. He considers the following options:

- *Action A:* Refuse to get involved and state, "This is not administration's problem."

- *Action B:* Tell Dr. Hursh that he is being unreasonable and that the service-learning requirement is unrealistic.

- *Action C:* Schedule a meeting with Dr. Hursh and his students to discuss this dilemma and actively facilitate a solution.

- *Action D:* Support Dr. Hursh and ask him to meet with his students to reach a mutually agreeable solution.

Step 4: Determine and Analyze the Consequences for Each Proposed Course of Action

Action A: Refuse to get involved and state, "This is not administration's problem."

Positive. This option is perhaps the easiest for the vice president because he could remain neutral in the dispute between faculty and students. In addition, by not becoming involved, he could support faculty academic freedom.

Negative. The vice president could refuse to get involved, but his academic vision, mission, and goals would not be met by ignoring this dilemma. Part of an administrator's mission is to ensure that they are empowering students and faculty to contribute to the community and to support service-learning as a legitimate academic enterprise.

Action B: Tell Dr. Hursh that he is being unreasonable and that the service-learning requirement is unrealistic.

Positive. Like Action A, this option appears to the vice president to be a way to placate students and, at the same time, deal with Dr. Hursh. Dr. Hursh's students would be pleased with this solution and would have their request answered.

Negative. As in Action A, part of the institution's academic mission is to provide support services for faculty and students in order to encourage participation in the community. However, micromanaging Dr. Hursh's course requirements would be an infringement upon Dr. Hursh's academic freedom.

Action C: Schedule a meeting with Dr. Hursh and his students to discuss this dilemma and actively facilitate a solution.

Positive. As long as all parties are amenable to this discussion and willing to accept the solution, this is a tenable option. This option would give Dr. Hursh and his students with an opportunity to give voice to their views. It would also provide a venue for forthright discussion on potential solutions to this dilemma.

Negative. The vice president would be concerned about violating academic freedom and about the amount of time required to reach a solution.

Additionally, taking this action could needlessly involve the union and aggravate an existing adversarial relationship.

Action D: Support Dr. Hursh and ask him to work with his students to reach a mutually agreeable solution.

Positive. This option would preserve Dr. Hursh's academic freedom and give Dr. Hursh and his students an opportunity to fully discuss their differences and resolve this dilemma. Perhaps through further dialogue both parties could come to appreciate and understand the two sides of this dilemma and engage in effective consensus-building and conflict resolution strategies involving compromise and cooperation.

Negative. This course of action might be risky since Dr. Hursh and his students were not previously able to reach a consensus. And, since the vice president is unwilling to take an active role in supporting and modeling the importance of civic responsibility and engagement, Dr. Hursh may continue to believe that his efforts at effective pedagogy and service in the community are unsupported. The vice president is concerned that Dr. Hursh believes his extra effort is unproductive and fruitless. Ultimately, this strategy might result in a negative relationship between Dr. Hursh and the vice president, as well as between Dr. Hursh and his students.

Step 5: Decide on the Best Course of Action

The vice president chooses Action D. He asks Dr. Hursh to meet with his students to discuss the best solution for all concerned. He makes this decision because he believes it is most important that he support Dr. Hursh's academic freedom.

Step 6: Evaluate and Reflect on the Decision

The vice president hopes that Dr. Hursh will appreciate his decision to support whatever resolution Dr. Hursh reaches with the students. He feels this solution will encourage students to engage in effective conflict resolution and will provide an opportunity to explore a real-world dilemma in a safe environment. The vice president realizes the need to reconsider the commitment to the strategic vision and mission of the college.

Applying the pillow, newspaper, and child tests, the vice president believes that he has made a decision that meets the needs of both Dr. Hursh and his students. Taking into consideration available information and the best interests of all, the vice president is comfortable with his decision, would see no problem in having this discussed in the newspaper, and would not be reluctant to discuss this dilemma and solution with his children.

Related Issues

Instituting a practice of designating service-learning courses prior to registration provides students with important information about course requirements. Students can then develop academic and personal schedules based on this knowledge. In addition, they will be better prepared to engage with the community.

On the other hand, because colleges and universities offer a large number of courses per semester, designating service-learning courses would require additional resources. Some faculty and administrators might be concerned that some service-learning courses could be missed during the identification process. As with most changes to college and university practices, there could be some early resistance and challenges. Therefore, ensuring that all departments comply with this request could be a long and tedious process. Some department chairs might argue that identifying service-learning courses is yet another task that adds to their workload. In addition, it may be unfair to require a special designation for service-learning courses only. It could be argued that, for example, math-intensive and writing-intensive courses should also be designated. Lastly, since most schedules are built six to nine months in advance, it is difficult to respond to changing community needs or requests.

Additional Dilemma

Dr. Dorn, the new dean of academic affairs, has been hired at a small private college. She spent the previous month learning about the characteristics of the college, the services offered, and its needs. The job seems very promising, but she has discovered a challenge. The budget was approved prior to her arrival and, in general, looks fine, but Dr. Dorn is concerned about the money available for faculty training. Faculty have articulated interest in learning more about service-learning. On the other hand, the college recently invested in upgrades to the technology related to teaching. The college purchased an educational package for the faculty to use in the management of their courses. Both are important areas of faculty development. Faculty identified service-learning as an area of interest, but additional training in computer technology would also improve faculty teaching and student learning. The academic affairs budget does not allow for these two different areas of faculty training. Which one should be done first, considering that the other would not happen for at least a year?

1) Identify the ethical dilemma.

2) Why is it an ethical dilemma? Identify the relevant codes.

3) Identify and list information you think would be helpful in making a decision.

4) List at least three possible solutions to this dilemma.

5) Which of the proposed solutions would you choose?

6) Why would you choose this solution?

7) How would you evaluate whether this is a good solution?

Chapter Sixteen

Administrator Commitment
to Service-Learning

Tate College is a small, church-affiliated institution. In the college's mission statement is a mandate for both students and faculty to engage in service to the community. One way the college has sought to fulfill the mission is through service-learning. The college has a service-learning coordinator who works with faculty to identify potential service-learning opportunities. As part of this process, the coordinator screens agencies to ensure that they meet the criteria for service-learning partnerships with the college. These criteria require that the agencies include sufficient supervision and training, established polices and procedures, and a plan for the service-learning project that seems viable and of potential benefit to the students in terms of learning outcomes.

An administrator from a neighborhood citizens' group contacts the coordinator and expresses interest in working with an instructor and students on a project. The citizens' group was formed to identify, initiate, and maintain revitalization efforts for the neighborhood, which is one of the most poverty-stricken areas of the city in which the college is located. It is characterized by a large number of unoccupied buildings, absentee-landlord residences, homeless persons, drug dealers, and other crime.

For their first step to improve their community, the members of the citizens' group want to conduct a community assets survey of the neighborhood residents. This survey will ask residents to report demographic information, resources they possess, perceptions of problems in the neighborhood, and assets they desire for the neighborhood, such as a bank or crime-watch group. The citizens hope that through a partnership with the college, they will be able to work with an instructor and students who can provide assistance with survey instrument design, methodological procedures, data collection, and data analysis. In turn, they believe this project would be a valuable learning experience for students.

The college service-learning coordinator is enthusiastic about the project, and identifies a faculty member in the political science department who specializes in grassroots organizations. The faculty member is very interested and believes that this project would be an excellent service-learning opportunity for his intermediate-level course on community organizations. He believes that the project will give students a better understanding of the processes and structure of grassroots organizations, barriers to such organizations' sustainability and impact, and the methodological skills characteristic of social science inquiry. In addition, the faculty member recognizes the benefit that this service-learning project will provide for the organization and the community as a whole. He predicts that students will gain a greater appreciation for the value of civic engagement, which is an educational goal not only for his department but also for the college, as reflected in its mission statement. The faculty member plans to offer the course for the upcoming semester.

After a few meetings between representatives of the neighborhood revitalization group and the faculty member, facilitated by the service-learning coordinator, the parameters of the service-learning project are delineated. Students will go door-to-door asking residents to complete the survey via an interview. To the greatest extent possible, students will be accompanied by community residents who are members of the revitalization group, although this may not always be possible due to scheduling conflicts.

The service-learning coordinator, as part of her job responsibilities, sends a periodic report to the academic dean of the college. This report presents the service-learning projects planned for the upcoming semester, including identification of the involved parties and a description of each project. After reading the report, the dean of the college becomes concerned about this particular undertaking. The dean believes that the possible physical danger to students is great. Yet he recognizes the enormous benefit that the project would bring to the community and the students. He realizes that the college has already made a commitment to the community, and to break that commitment would not benefit the college's positive relationship with the community. Further, faculty are encouraged to include service-learning in their teaching; the dean is unsure if it is appropriate for him to tell a faculty member who has taken the initiative to include a service-learning project in his course that the dean cannot support this undertaking.

Step 1: Identify and Define the Dilemma

Several codes are in conflict in this dilemma, especially with regard to Section III of the SLC. First, SLC III.1 states that administrators must *recognize and support opportunities for service-learning as part of a liberal education.* This code is clearly reflected in Tate College's mission. Administrators also have the responsibility to *be sensitive to and knowledgeable about community needs* (SLC III.3). The service-learning coordinator, as part of her duties as a college administrator, has adhered to both of these codes through her development and support of the partnership between the neighborhood revitalization group and the faculty member. The dean must also adhere to these codes and support the community initiative to address problems in the neighborhood, as well as the faculty member's willingness to support the college's mission. A breach of this verbal contract would create tension and ill will between the college and the community group. The negative impact could go well beyond relations with this one agency and have a detrimental impact on other community groups' relationships with the college, other faculty members' willingness to incorporate service-learning into their curriculum, and the service-learning coordinator's initiative to establish these partnerships. However, the dean also *must make every effort to minimize risky and unsafe locations and circumstances* (SLC III.4). The dean is concerned that the students might find themselves in dangerous situations that they are unprepared to handle. The dean faces a dilemma of whether to allow the project to continue or to terminate it.

Step 2: Address Relevant Principles and Gather Information

First, the college embraces the principle of beneficence as part of its mission statement. This service-learning opportunity provides an excellent way for the faculty member and the students to fulfill this mission. Through identification of both the assets and needs of the community, the neighborhood revitalization group will have the information necessary to seek funding and political change to improve the quality of life for the neighborhood residents. Similarly, the dean also is bound to the principle of nonmaleficence, which includes "protecting from harm." Thus, the dean is obligated to protect the students from harm. Allowing this service-learning project to proceed may put the students in harm's way. The principle of fidelity/responsibility is also relevant to this dilemma. The service-learning coordinator and the faculty member have already made a commitment to the neighborhood citizens group, and the organization has been working with the college for the past month. At this point, having to begin again, especially without free assistance, would result in a severe setback to the group.

With regard to gathering information, the dean should call a meeting of the involved parties before making any decisions: the service-learning coordinator, the faculty member, and representatives from the neighborhood revitalization group. At this meeting, the dean could seek detailed and extensive information regarding the extent and reality of the potential risks. Is the dean letting media sensationalism bias his perspective? Is he being too risk-aversive due to liability concerns? He should be very clear on the details of what the project would entail, especially in terms of the students, activities, and the supervision of the students. The dean should consider visiting the neighborhood and meeting with some of the residents. He should then express his concerns and explain the liability and ethical issues involved (SLC III.5).

Another excellent source of information would be administrators from other colleges that have strong service-learning initiatives. How have they dealt with similar situations? What protections have they put in place to minimize risks to students' safety? Has there ever been an event where a student was harmed while participating in a similar service-learning experience?

Step 3: Propose Courses of Action

The dean considers three possible courses of action:

- *Action A:* Allow the project to proceed as planned.

- *Action B:* Cancel the project.

- *Action C:* Request reconsideration of areas of concern and seek possible alternatives.

Step 4: Determine and Analyze the Consequences for Each Proposed Course of Action

Action A: Allow the project to proceed as planned.

Positive. If the dean chooses this course of action, he would be honoring the academic freedom of the faculty member and the verbal agreement the college has made with the revitalization group, and he would not be micromanaging the service-learning coordinator's area of responsibility. Also, the positive benefits of the service-learning project to the students and the community would be realized.

Negative. By allowing the project to proceed as planned, the dean would not be taking responsibility for his concerns about the students' safety. By merely hoping that nothing bad happens, he is surely not taking an active enough role. This may be a choice he would deeply regret, should any of his concerns be realized.

Action B: Cancel the project.

Positive. This choice addresses the dean's concerns by eliminating exposure of students to a potentially dangerous situation.

Negative. If the project is canceled, the positive benefits to the students and the community would not be realized. The college would breach a verbal contract it has made with the citizens' group. This would damage the college's relationship with the community, and be counter to the college's mission. To cancel the partnership at this point would severely set back the citizens' group's progress. Given the often tenuous viability of these groups, forward momentum is critical to their sustainability. The faculty member has already structured his entire course around the inclusion of the service-learning project. It would be extremely difficult to restructure the course without the project in the short period of time remaining. Perhaps the most important consequence would be that the faculty member might view the dean's action as a breach of academic freedom. Similarly, the service learning coordinator might feel some resentment for the dean's intrusion into her area of responsibility. She might also be less willing to consider future service-learning projects that entail any elements of risk.

Action C: Request reconsideration of areas of concern and seek possible alternatives.

Positive. By calling the meeting proposed in Step 2, the dean would be taking an active role in and responsibility for the project. Although not necessarily sanctioning the project, he would be demonstrating his willingness to consider the possibility of moving forward, should he feel comfortable that the risk to the students could be minimized. If the project could continue with modifications, the service-learning benefits could still be achieved. The faculty member would not have to redesign his course and might not feel any threat to his academic freedom. The faculty member would likely appreciate the dean's concern and support. Finally, the college might be able to uphold its commitment to the organization and adhere to its mission statement.

Negative. The service-learning coordinator, faculty member, and even the organization representatives might still perceive this solution as micromanagement and an impingement on academic freedom. Also, it is possible that acceptable solutions could not be agreed upon and that the project would have to be terminated anyway. In the end, this might only further delay the faculty member's planning and cause even greater hardship for the citizens group.

Step 5: Decide on the Best Course of Action

The dean decides to take Action C: request reconsideration of areas of concern and seek possible solutions. The dean meets with the faculty member, the service-learning coordinator, and a representative from the citizens' group to discuss his concerns. The dean explains his apprehension regarding student safety and expresses his interest in possible measures to address those concerns. He presents information regarding the college's liability, should a student come into harm's way. Since this is a school-related activity, the college's insurance policy would cover the students while they are engaged in the service-learning activity. However, if the insurance company has to cover the cost of injury to a student, it would seriously impact the cost of insurance for the college. A severe claim could possibly jeopardize the college's ability to secure insurance.

In light of these concerns, the involved parties agree to certain steps. First, the service-learning coordinator offers to arrange a safety workshop for the students, provided by the college security personnel. This is consistent with SLC III.6: *provide faculty with opportunities for training and education in service-learning curriculum infusion,* and SLC II.5: *properly train and inform students of the responsibilities and potential risks prior to the beginning of the service-learning activity.* The faculty member agrees to include this training in one of the class meetings. Second, everyone agrees that members of the neighborhood citizens' group must accompany students. All interviews will take place late in the morning, the time during which crime is at its lowest level, according to the group's representatives. Also, a plan is developed for how students and residents should deal with any problem situations that might arise.

Step 6: Evaluate and Reflect on the Decision

Action C has fewer predicted drawbacks than the other proposed courses of action. Although the possibility of not reaching acceptable solutions is a serious risk, at least a good-faith attempt is being made, which will be appreciated more than a flat denial without dialogue among the involved parties. The steps taken to address these concerns will increase the burden on group members, which may ultimately reduce the number of homes visited and thus the response rate; however, that decrease is a reasonable cost. Lastly, some citizens' group members might resent the dean's decision. That is, they may feel the dean has a misperception about their neighborhood and feel that he is overreacting and disrespectful about their community.

Does this decision pass the pillow, newspaper, and child tests? The dean is very concerned about the students' safety and will not rest easy until the project is completed and no harm has come to students. Just based on the pillow test, denial of the project altogether seems the best option. The newspaper test may lead the dean to the same conclusion. The dean envisions the negative press that would occur if a student were harmed. However, the dean also believes that negative press would occur if the college backs out of the project at this late date. The community group would be resentful and might use the press to tell the public that they believe the college failed to honor an agreement due to a negative opinion of their community. Finally, the dean believes the decision he made is most consistent with the values he is trying to uphold and feels it meets the child test.

Related Issues

This dilemma raises the question of the extent to which instructors and service-learning coordinators have autonomy in decision-making with regard to service-learning projects. Should academic institutions have a policy of requiring a senior administrator or even the board—as the individual or individuals ultimately responsible for the safety of the students—to have final approval of such projects? One could argue that such a policy would infringe upon academic freedom. Senior administrators do not need to approve other course requirements, so why should service-learning be an exception? If approvals are justifiable due to the unique challenges presented by service-learning opportunities, then on what criteria should such decisions be made? An approval policy would have to be carefully crafted to achieve the dual goals of securing the approval of a senior administrator and preserving the faculty's autonomy.

This dilemma shows the risk inherent in virtually all service-learning projects. Placing students into the community puts them at risk, whether the risks are environmental exposure, crime, disease, or negative social interactions. One way to assess whether a risk is reasonable or justifiable is to weigh it against the potential benefits of the service-learning experience. The difficulty in such an assessment is that the risk in the current case is only a potential one. If serious harm were to come to a student, then no benefit would justify that occurrence. However, if the potential for an adverse event to occur is minimal, then the risk may be outweighed by the benefit to the students in terms of learning outcomes and civic engagement. Another way to approach the risk question is to ask whether the risk posed is any greater than that which a student might normally expect to encounter in his or her daily life. We all face risk of harm as we carry out our daily activities and responsibilities. We could become random targets of crime, be exposed to infectious diseases, become targets of verbal criticism, or be exposed to other risks. By engaging in a service-learning experience, are students subjected to any greater risk than they typically encounter? If the answer is no, then one may say the risk is reasonable and justifiable. If the answer is yes, then the risks outweigh the benefits of the service-learning experience, and it should either not be undertaken, or it should be modified to diminish the risk significantly. The issue of risk management is discussed further in Chapter 20.

Additional Dilemma

Mark is an environmental studies major with a focus on freshwater ecology. Mark's college has recently formed a partnership with a civic organization that is working to restore the town's waterfront. The instructor for Mark's hydrology course has developed a service-learning project to help the waterfront restoration group . The project entails taking several water samples from the lake to determine the quality of the water. Previous testing has indicated dangerously elevated bacteria levels due to local farming runoff. Should the project proceed?

1) Identify the ethical dilemma.

2) Why do we have ethical dilemmas? Identify the relevant rules.

3) Identify and list information you think would be helpful in making a decision.

4) List at least three possible solutions to this dilemma.

5) Which of the proposed solutions would you choose?

6) Why would you choose this solution?

7) How would you evaluate whether this is a good solution?

Chapter Seventeen

Treat All Constituents in a Manner Consistent With Ethical Principles

C ommunity engagement has received special attention in recent years; in particular, research has been conducted to understand whether and how service relates to civic engagement. Consider an example in which a public museum, as part of a community outreach program, is planning an exhibit that would educate the public on civic engagement. The museum has identified a granting agency that may provide funding for the exhibit. The museum has asked a local college to assist with research needed for the grant proposal.

During the planning for the exhibit, the museum director contacts the service-learning program coordinator for the college. Since the program coordinator is new to the college, she asks the academic dean, Dr. Lorna, for suggestions. Dr. Lorna, a major supporter of academic service-learning, is very enthusiastic about this project because of the benefits that service-learning experiences bring to the students and the community. When she learns about the grant request, she jumps at the chance to cooperate with the museum. She tells the program coordinator that there will be a course offered the following semester that is perfect for the project. She offers to contact the professor who teaches the course.

Dr. Lorna calls Dr. Martin to discuss the museum's grant-writing project. Dr. Martin, who is also new to the college, is the professor assigned to teach the capstone course in the political science department in the upcoming semester. Dr. Lorna tells Dr. Martin that the museum needs the grant for a new exhibit and tells him that his capstone course is perfect for the project and that she cannot think of any other course that would be suitable. She would like to volunteer his class to do the grant-writing for the museum exhibit.

Dr. Martin is not familiar with service-learning and does not feel comfortable incorporating it into his course. Besides, he has already prepared the syllabus for the course and is looking forward to teaching the course with different projects, none of which involve a service component. Dr. Lorna is a little surprised by his reluctance but brushes it aside. She explains how the service-learning coordinator could help him, and explains all the benefits that the students and the community would receive from the project. She also mentions that the deadlines fit well with the college schedule and that the administration would be supportive of this service-learning project.

Dr. Martin understands the importance of the project for the college and promises to think about it. A few days later, the chair of the political science department calls Dr. Lorna to explain that the department currently has plans that cannot accommodate new projects, especially service-learning experiences, but that the department would be glad to discuss such possibilities for the future.

Dr. Lorna did not expect that response. She feels that the faculty and the department are not supportive of service-learning or the institutionalization of civic engagement. Since she cannot think of another course that would be appropriate for the project, what should she do?

Step 1: Identify and Define the dilemma

Dr. Lorna is so enthusiastic about academic service-learning benefits to the students and community that she has created a difficult situation for herself. She is *sensitive to and knowledgeable about the community needs* (SLC II1.3), and yet her enthusiasm has led her to volunteer a course for which she is not directly responsible, violating SLC II1.7: to *treat all constituents in a manner consistent with ethical principles.*

Dr. Lorna only realized there was a problem when she talked to Dr. Martin, and he explained that he had already planned the course with no service-learning assignment. By then, she had already told the coordinator for service-learning that she had the perfect course to write the grant for the museum exhibit. Furthermore, the coordinator had already confirmed the project with the museum director. Dr. Lorna reviews the course schedule and finds that there are no other courses being offered that semester that would be able to incorporate the service-learning project. If faculty does not support administrators in their attempts to institutionalize service-learning, what is the administration to do? What should Dr. Lorna do?

Step 2: Address Relevant Principles and Gather Information

By looking at the principles proposed in Chapter 1, Dr. Lorna realizes that she did not follow the principle of autonomy and respect for people's rights. In this case, she did not expect the professor to reject her suggestion and select his own method for teaching the course. And, even though she is a supporter of service-learning, she should not allow her enthusiasm to interfere with academic freedom. She should find other ways to let the faculty know about community needs and let them address those needs as they see fit. However, she still has the responsibility to support the request since she had assumed there was a course that would be a perfect fit with the project. Dr. Lorna reviews the schedule of courses again and cannot identify another course that would fulfill the needs of the project. She also checks with the service-learning coordinator. To her dismay, she finds out that the museum is looking forward to working on the project with the students.

Step 3: Propose Courses of Action

Dr. Lorna is not sure what she should do. She considers the following options:

- *Action A:* Announce the service-learning project to the whole faculty and wait for a volunteer.

- *Action B:* Contact the museum and cancel the support for the project.

- *Action C:* Find other ways to support the museum request.

Step 4: Determine and Analyze the Consequences for Each Proposed Course of Action

Action A: Announce the service-learning project to the whole faculty and wait for a volunteer.

Positive. Dr. Lorna could make the announcement to the whole faculty, as she should have done initially, and wait for a volunteer. If a faculty member volunteers, that would benefit all parties: the college, the museum, and the faculty and students working on the project.

Negative. Since no other course seemed appropriate for the project, there is a chance that no faculty will step forward to use the grant-writing project as a service-learning experience for the upcoming semester.

Action B: Contact the museum and cancel the support for the project.

Positive. Dr. Lorna would acknowledge academic freedom and allow the faculty to select assignments as they see fit for the purposes of the courses they teach.

Negative. The museum would not get the support for the grant writing, which might affect the preparation of the exhibit on civic engagement, and might affect the public relations with the college.

Action C: Find other ways to support the museum request.

Positive. By looking for alternatives to the service-learning experience, Dr. Lorna would support the museum's request and maintain a positive relationship with them. She would need to consider creating an internship, work-study, research assistantship, or a faculty position and determine which alternative would benefit both the college and the museum. She could also consider teaching a course that would incorporate the service-learning experience.

Negative. Since she already reviewed the schedule of courses and could not find one that is appropriate for the project, the internship probably would not fulfill any other course's objectives. Instead, she might need to create a research assistantship or work-study position. However, either one would be costly for the college. If she decides to teach a new course herself, she might not find students who are interested in registering for a course that was not in the schedule.

Step 5: Decide on the Best Course of Action

Dr. Lorna decides that Actions A and C are not mutually exclusive. She decides to take Action A: announce the project to the whole faculty and wait for a volunteer, but make it an open invitation for faculty to consider not only service-learning in their courses but also the options she considered in Action C. She asks for faculty who might be interested in assisting with the project by adding a service-learning component, internship, or research assistantship. If someone volunteers, all would be well, and she could inform the museum of the possibility of having the grant-writing done by students or faculty members at the college. However, if no one volunteers, she would need to report to the museum staff that she asked the faculty for assistance but no one was available to include the project in courses for the upcoming semester.

Step 6: Evaluate and Reflect on the Decision

Dr. Lorna feels that her decision will benefit everyone. She will allow the faculty to freely select the grant-writing project if it fits with a course's objective. She will allow the grant-writing project to be selected under a format that benefits a particular course. She will be able to identify the outcome of her decision at the end of the deadline given to the faculty. Providing information to the faculty and allowing them to make a decision might lead to better outcomes than selecting one course and informing the professor of the benefits such a project would have on the students.

    If such an experience is not feasible this semester, then Dr. Lorna will have to inform the museum director and hope for a better chance of cooperation next time. She feels comfortable with the pillow, newspaper, and child tests: she can sleep with her decision, she would not mind seeing it on the front page of the paper, and she would tell her child to do the same thing that she has done.

Additional Dilemma

A college received a lot of publicity for the positive results of several service-learning projects that helped the community. As a result, many agencies in town have asked the college to support their needs. The college was suddenly overwhelmed by the number of requests. As the administrators sort through the requests, they realize that some of them are beyond the support the college can offer. However, some of the requestors were the first to contact the college.

1) Identify the ethical dilemma.

2) Why is it an ethical dilemma? Identify the relevant codes.

3) Identify and list information you think would be helpful in making a decision.

4) List at least three possible solutions to this dilemma.

5) Which of the proposed solutions would you choose?

6) Why would you choose this solution?

7) How would you evaluate whether this is a good solution?

Chapter Eighteen

Allocation of Institutional Resources and Service-Learning Implementation

D r. Myers, the provost of a large northwestern state university, has received a request for funding and transportation support for a service-learning project developed in the engineering department. This proposal was submitted in the spring semester by Dr. Brown, who has been teaching an Introduction to Landscaping Design class for the past 15 years. Dr. Brown has included a service-learning component in this course for the last eight years. For the upcoming fall semester, students in this class will be required to travel 15 miles into the inner city during the semester to perform a total of 40 service hours. Service-learners will be asked to beautify one inner city block by planting trees, cleaning sidewalks, and removing graffiti. They will also create a community garden and decide where sidewalk lights should be placed. This project will require cost sharing by property owners, the university, and the local energy company. Because this will require a long-term commitment from everyone involved, Dr. Brown also wants to perform outcome assessments.

The university's mission statement and general education requirement stress decision-making based on moral and ethical considerations as well as the importance and value of involvement in the local community. The university has historically supported off-campus activities, in-class integration of service-learning, and encouraged students to be culturally aware and civically engaged. However, the university faces fiscal difficulties because of cuts in state funding. Because of this budget shortfall, administrators have been making difficult and often unpopular decisions. This has created an adversarial relationship between faculty and administrators and an unwillingness to work together for the common good of students and the larger community.

Dr. Myers and Dr. Brown meet to discuss Dr. Brown's need for institutional support and resources for this community service-learning activity. Dr. Brown has requested that his department chair also be present, but the chair feels Dr. Brown has the experience and expertise to adequately present his case without the chair's presence. At the meeting, Dr. Brown explains that he was aware that the university had eliminated the coordinator of service-learning position to cut nonessential service, but that he was not aware of other cost-cutting measures. Dr. Myers replies that the university is experiencing serious budget problems and so it is unlikely that institutional vehicles, transportation expenses, or campus supplies and resources can be allocated for service-learning activities. Dr. Brown reminds Dr. Myers that he made a commitment to the community members of this particular block and believes that these activities will benefit students, the university's relations with the community, and the inner city and its residents.

Dr. Myers is initially unsure how this request should be handled, particularly since he wants to fairly and equitably address the resource requests on the campus. As provost, he must frequently make difficult and unpopular decisions as he considers the best interests of the entire university community. Dr. Myers decides he can only fund one financial request for the upcoming semester. Prior to Dr. Brown's request, he was seriously considering a plan to update a small computer lab on campus. If he uses available resources to refurbish the lab, he will be unable to support Dr. Brown's students and activities in the community.

Dr. Myers needs to determine which option will most benefit students and the university. Regardless of his decision, he will need to provide outcome measures to the president of the university and to the state system office. In other words, he needs to justify not only his decision, but also its value-added component to students, faculty, the university, and the larger community.

Step 1: Identify and Define the Dilemma

Dr. Myers has faced similar requests for funding in the past but has always been able to arrive at a compromise among faculty, students, and community needs. However, with decreasing tuition reimbursement programs, uncertain business support, and higher operating costs, Dr. Myers must carefully consider the consequences of the decisions he makes. Therefore, several service-learning codes are in conflict. The university has historically provided *mechanisms for the institutionalization of civic engagement* (SLC III.2) and is *sensitive to and knowledgeable about community needs* (SLC III.3). But, at the same time, with a decision against service-learning, Dr. Myers will fail to provide resources to honor the university's commitment to *appropriate service-learning experiences as part of a liberal education* (SLC III.1). Further, if Dr. Myers is unwilling to support Dr. Brown's request, he sends the message to students, faculty, and members of the larger community that support for and involvement in the community are not valued by the university.

On the other hand, if Dr. Myers allocates the needed resources for this off-campus service, then he may be criticized for neglecting student computer needs on campus. He has frequently heard negative comments from students and parents about the lack of updated and efficient computer technology. Although it would be a small step, using these funds for modernizing one of the campus computer labs would be a move toward improvement of campus resources for students. Dr. Myers must weigh the consequences of both courses of action.

Step 2: Address Relevant Principles and Gather Information

Beneficence is a relevant principle, regardless of the decision Dr. Myers makes. In reviewing his obligations to on-campus students, Dr. Myers considers designating available funds to update the small computer lab. This would afford students an opportunity to use the most efficient and latest technology for class assignments and would help prepare students for future employment. On the other hand, Dr. Myers would also be promoting the good of others if he decides to support student activities in the local community. This would enhance the university's image as a caring and involved partner with the community and would provide students with experiences in civic engagement.

Dr. Myers is well aware that positive off-campus activities cultivate leadership skills among students and enhance student self-esteem and future citizenship behavior. Giving back to the community not only develops connections but also improves the quality of life for local residents.

In an effort to gather as much information as possible, Dr. Myers meets with the dean's council, the chair of the engineering department, several community leaders, and members of the university's foundation board. Through this process, he hopes to find a viable solution to this dilemma. Although they do not provide a definite solution, these conversations help Dr. Myers clarify his thinking.

Step 3: Propose Courses of Action

The next step in the decision-making process involves identifying various courses of action. Dr. Myers is faced with a difficult decision. Students will benefit whether a lab is updated or the service-learning project is supported. Dr. Myers believes more students would profit from an updated computer lab, but he also recognizes the university's commitment to the community and to faculty and students engaged in service-learning. He considers the following options:

- *Action A:* Provide no financial resources for this activity and instead update the small computer lab.

- *Action B:* Ask the engineering department to underwrite the cost of this service-learning activity. Also contact the math department and request student and faculty assistance to develop an assessment tool for the project and the community.

- *Action C:* Ask the community and energy company to underwrite these costs.

- *Action D:* Request support from the foundation board or other grant-funding departments on campus.

- *Action E:* Provide financial resources and vehicles for this activity and delay upgrading the computer lab until next year.

Step 4: Determine and Analyze the Consequences for Each Proposed Course of Action

Action A: Provide no financial resources for this activity and instead update the small computer lab.

Positive. Because of the serious resource needs of the university and the limited available funds, Dr. Myers believes upgrading the computer lab is the best solution. At the dean's council, two of the four academic deans voiced concern about inadequate technology support on campus. The computer lab is used by students from a variety of disciplines. Students report that these computers are either not working or are extremely slow and unable to handle the addition of new software. Dr. Myers is convinced that this would be a wise and practical use of funds and that the decision would benefit students and several academic departments on campus.

Negative. Since the university has historically supported activities in the community and a vision for student service, an unwillingness to honor this commitment sends the message to students, faculty, and neighborhood residents that service to the community is not valued by the university and its administration.

In addition, if Dr. Brown decides to fulfill this obligation, he would be making an enormous personal commitment of time and energy to ensure that monetary support is secured from other sources and that students are provided appropriate transportation options for the service-learning project. Dr. Brown would regularly need to drive some students himself and ask other students to provide their own transportation. In the long run, this could be a costly mistake, as there are potential insurance risks and also time management issues for Dr. Brown.

Action B: Ask the engineering department to underwrite the cost of this service-learning activity. Also contact the math department and request student and faculty assistance to develop an assessment tool for the project and the community.

Positive. This option would provide a solution to this dilemma that would free up the needed monies for updating the computer lab. Also, students in the math department would benefit from hands-on experience with survey/questionnaire development.

Negative. Unfortunately, after checking resource statements, it is clear to Dr. Myers that the engineering department has limited funds with which to underwrite this project. Funding the project would require the department to abandon several of its pressing needs. In the end, this would further fracture the already difficult relationship between the engineering department and several administrators. As far as the math department's contributions, this directive could also contribute to the existing tenuous relationship. The department's chair and faculty might feel besieged by additional unsolicited and unsupported work.

Action C: Ask the community and energy company to underwrite these costs.

Positive. This option would enable the university's administrators to allocate the necessary funds for updating the computer lab and would also empower the community and local energy company. Collaboration within the community would improve relations and provide a sense of control over the various projects. This would be good advertising for the energy company as it partners with the community to provide residents with a safer and more pleasant environment.

Negative. A failure of the university to meet its commitment to the community could be misread as a lack of interest in the residents. The beautification plan is viewed as a collaborative effort among the university, community, and energy company, and any change in that arrangement could seriously impact the reputation of the university and its relationships. A change in the arrangement could also perpetuate any stereotypes about the academic community as being unwilling and unable to remain focused on their promises and share their resources.

Action D: Request support from the foundation board or other grant-funding departments on campus.

Positive. As in Actions A, B, and C, this option would relieve the university of its financial burden to the community and would enable it to renovate the computer lab.

Negative. Application for these resources through campus funding sources would require a considerable amount of planning and lead time. Therefore, this would only prove to be a viable alternative from a long-term perspective. In essence, it would not be feasible to anticipate funding support in time to initiate and complete the project. This option would require an investigation into available grants, qualifications, and money allocations. In the long run, it is possible there would be no campus funding sources to underwrite this endeavor.

Action E: Provide financial resources and vehicles for this activity and delay upgrading the computer lab until next year.

Positive. This option would provide Dr. Brown with the needed funds to meet his and the university's commitment to the community. These activities would not only enhance the community but also expose students to a variety of useful experiences. If successful, the outcome would improve the image of the university and resident-university relations.

Negative. The university's and students' best interests might not be served by honoring this commitment. Would a greater number of students be served with a newly renovated computer lab? By failing to provide the latest in computer technology, the university's administrators could be criticized for neglecting student needs. This remains a difficult decision.

Step 5: Decide on the Best Course of Action

Dr. Myers consults with a variety of constituents on campus and reviews the university's mission. According to its vision statement, the university is dedicated to excellence in learning and teaching. This commitment involves the intellectual, social, and ethical development of students through the provision of high quality programs and opportunities. Partnerships and collaboration are recommended to prepare students to be global citizens. Another goal of the university is to train students to effectively use technologies to enhance knowledge acquisition and learning.

With this in mind, Dr. Myers chooses Action A and allocates the funds for updating the computer lab. He believes this will serve the best interests of the university, its students, and the various departments using the lab. This decision should create the least amount of negative feedback from other administrators, deans, and faculty.

Step 6: Evaluate and Reflect on the Decision

Dr. Myers wants to ensure the optimal use of resources and provide mechanisms for the continuance of service to the community. At the same time, he prefers a proactive rather than reactive decision-making process. As he reviews the positive and negative consequences of the courses of action available to him, Dr. Myers recognizes that a short-term solution will not solve the larger issue of the university's responsibilities to students, faculty, and community. He reminds himself that any allocation of resources must serve the most individuals and should ultimately be driven by the university's mission and goals.

Using the pillow, newspaper, and child tests, Dr. Myers is confident that his decision reflects a sound and rational judgment that he would not lose sleep over, and that the decision could be published in the college newspaper honestly and effectively. He would not be troubled about explaining and justifying his decision to his children and grandchildren.

Related Issues

As educational institutions are expected to continue providing services with less funding and resources, they will need to clearly articulate goals, missions, and values. Adherence to core objectives can provide a framework for addressing informed decisions about roles in the community and responsibilities to students and faculty. The harsh reality of continuing budget cuts, reallocation of funds, and personnel shortages can create barriers to service in the community that require creative solutions and innovative strategies.

Academic and institutional policies established by college and university administrators need to incorporate contingency plans to address budget shortfalls. The ongoing achievement of mission and goals requires a creative readiness to reallocate resources, solicit new funding streams, and develop better strategies to manage fiscal uncertainties. In addition, faculty need to be informed of budget limitations so they do not make commitments that cannot be fulfilled. Faculty cannot continue to make connections with students and the community under the assumption that they will have the financial support of administration.

In the long run, continuous improvement of student educational experiences requires partnerships outside the institution. Therefore, if service-learning is an important mandate for a college or university, administrators need to develop collaborative relationships with public and private businesses and agencies to ensure that opportunities are available for students and faculty to enhance academic experiences and build citizenship behavior.

Additional Dilemma

Henderson College is a small religiously-affiliated institution located in a somewhat impoverished community in the Midwestern section of the United States. As part of a continuing effort to coordinate academic and student services on campus, the college applied for and received a large service-learning grant to clean a local stream that runs through the town, paint and repair several houses, and provide other student services to local residents.

Interested faculty and the service-learning director attended several workshops provided by the granting agency on the incorporation of service-learning into the curriculum. However, when the faculty submitted carefully designed budgets for the resources needed to fulfill the grant and community needs, they were turned down by the school's administration and asked to reduce the amounts requested. As the faculty began to investigate and question, they found that much of the grant money would remain at the college for administrative programs and clerical services rather than for community use. During the instructional training provided by the granting agency, the faculty was told that approximately 5% of the grant would be used for administrative overhead.

1) Identify the ethical dilemma.

2) Why is it an ethical dilemma? Identify the relevant codes.

3) Identify and list information you think would be helpful in making a decision.

4) List at least three possible solutions to this dilemma.

5) Which of the proposed solutions would you choose?

6) Why would you choose this solution?

7) How would you evaluate whether this is a good solution?

PART V

Assessment and Risk Management

Chapter Nineteen

Assessment of
Service-Learning Code of Ethics

Because of an increasing public and governmental demand for accountability in higher education, assessment is heavily emphasized in the current academic culture and has become an essential component of any pedagogical method (Astin, 1991; Boud, 1990; Lazerson, Wagener, & Shumanis, 1999; Lissitz & Schafer, 2002; Shavelson & Huang, 2003). Accordingly, this chapter provides an overview of summative assessments of the goals of service-learning that have served as the focus of this text; namely, of civic engagement and its corollaries: democratic ideals such as tolerance and respect, justice, individual rights, and moral and value development. It also presents a way to conduct a formative assessment of adherence to the SLC. We stress, as before, that our objective in developing the SLC is not to mandate a particular set of values, but to provide a mechanism by which the goals of service learning might be more fully realized.

This chapter includes assessment techniques that apply to all service-learning practitioners—students, faculty, and administrators. The success of any service-learning program or individual project at any college or university requires the active, careful, and fully committed participation of all these campus constituents. Therefore, a comprehensive assessment approach will best show whether the goals of service-learning have been met. The approach should measure the extent to which students, faculty, and administrators followed the SLC over the course of the service-learning project.

Much of the enthusiasm for service-learning is predicated on the belief that it will provide many of the outcomes currently being emphasized in academe, especially value development and civic engagement

(Astin & Sax, 1998; Colby, Ehrlich, Beaumont, & Stephens, 2003; Giles & Eyler, 1994; Oates & Leavitt, 2003; Zlotkowski, 1998). We contend that such outcomes are much more likely to be achieved through active use of and adherence to the SLC. If all constituents involved in a service-learning project abide by the SLC, fewer ethical challenges will occur, and when they do, participants will be better able to resolve these dilemmas in ways that are consistent with ethical principles. This is an empirical argument, subject to assessment and validation. As one engages in service-learning opportunities, how does one determine that his or her goals have been met as a result of utilizing the SLC? Consistent with most current assessment practice, this question focuses on student outcomes, which fall into the category of summative assessment, or, measurement of final outcome.

There have been several outcome assessments of service-learning projects with regard to value development. In fact, some researchers have already assessed the extent to which service-learning results in moral growth (Boss, 1994; Cook, Hillman, & Carmer, 2003; Giles & Eyler, 1994; Gorman, Duffy, & Heffernan, 1994; Kendrick, 1996; Leming, 2001; Myers-Lipton, 1996), increased sense of civic responsibility (Astin & Sax, 1998; Giles & Eyler, 1994; Kendrick, 1996; Morgan & Streb, 2001; Myers-Lipton, 1996), and tolerance toward others (Bringle & Kremer, 1993; Eyler, Giles, & Braxton, 1997; Juhn et al., 1999; Morgan & Streb, 2001; Osborne, Hammerich, & Hensley, 1998). These studies rely heavily on established general measures of moral development, such as Kohlberg's (1981) Moral Interview or Rest's (1988) Defining Issues Test. Both of these scoring systems are designed to measure stages of moral development based upon Kohlberg's theory. It is beyond the scope of this book to discuss these measures in great detail; there are several comprehensive volumes on this subject that interested readers may consult (Colby et al., 1987a, 1987b; Gilligan, 1982; Kohlberg, 1971, 1981; Puka, 1994; Rest, 1990; Rest, Narvaez, Bebeau, & Thoma, 1999).

In addition to studies that measure the impact of service-learning on moral development, value development, and commitment to civic engagement, an increasing number of current resources guide one through the process of conducting an assessment in a service-learning project, including suggested methods and measures (Bringle, Phillips, & Hudson, 2004; Colby, Ehrlich, Beaumont, & Stephens, 2003; Eyler & Giles, 1999; Jacoby, 1996; Oates & Leavitt, 2003; Troppe, 1995).

Although many of these resources include questionnaires and similar quantitative measures, they emphasize the qualitative data found in students' reflective exercises. Since this is viewed as a critical component of the ethical decision-making model presented in this book, it seems that in order to see the impact of the SLC on these outcomes, one must closely examine the content of students' reflections, whether in oral or written format. Again, in addition to the aforementioned texts on service-learning assessment, there are several resources available on evaluating students' reflective exercises (Bringle & Hatcher, 1995; Marchel, 2004; National Service-Learning Clearinghouse, 2001). It is important to note that the vast majority of these measures have been largely focused on *student* outcomes. However, we encourage assessment of faculty, college-wide, and community outcomes of service-learning experiences. Although these topics are touched upon briefly in some of the resources already reviewed, there is a clear need for further development of assessment methods for these constituents. Standard methods of program evaluation (Gredler, 1996; Rossi, Freeman, & Lipsey, 1999) would be helpful resources when conducting summative assessment of faculty college-wide, and community outcomes of service-learning experiences.

The above collection of measures focuses primarily, if not exclusively, on *outcomes*. However, before one can measure the impact of the SLC on these outcomes, it is important to first establish that service-learning practitioners—students, faculty, and administrators—use the SLC while engaging in service-learning. This falls under the second category of assessment: formative or process assessment. This is an area that is also lacking in current service-learning assessment (Colby et al., 2003; Ehrlich, 2003; Lissitz & Schafer, 2002).

> If we are to go beyond participation rates and student self-assessments, we will need to develop observation procedures that document the processes of influence and instruments that capture more fully the important but less tangible psychological constructs such as moral identity and commitment, and performance variables such as critical thinking, negotiation, and effective communication. (Ehrlich, 2003, p. 8)

This almost exclusive focus on outcomes, as opposed to process, may be one of the reasons that tools such as the SLC have been overlooked in the student arena.

In the current context, formative assessment involves the question of the extent to which those engaging in service-learning behave in a manner consistent with the SLC. Three types of data would be useful in this regard: *behavioral observation, archival data,* and *self-report.* As Ehrlich (2003) states, one would ideally observe the individuals while they are engaged in the service-learning process to determine to what extent their behaviors adhere to the SLC. However, not all aspects of the SLC lend themselves to direct behavioral observation (e.g., *recognize and reflect upon potential challenges to their personal value systems,* SLC I.7).

One could conduct an analysis of any documents whose contents may serve as reliable indicators of adherence to the code. For example, a student's log of time spent at the service site, a faculty member's syllabus, and the administrative procedures established to support service-learning courses could all be used to this end.

The third type of data helpful for this formative evaluation is self-report. All those involved in the project, including the community agency's representatives and even clients, could be asked to rate both themselves and others on compliance with the code.

To help those who want to engage in this type of assessment, we have developed a set of questionnaires derived from the specific items in the SLC. Each question asks the respondent to indicate his or her level of agreement that the targeted service-learning practitioner (i.e., student, faculty, or administrator) fully adhered to that principle of the SLC. These questionnaires are included at the end of this chapter and may be used in the collection of all three types of data discussed: behavioral observation, archival analysis, and self-report.

One final issue is the utilization of the assessment results. Clearly, there is a variety of functions an assessment could serve. The ones held to be most valuable and consistent with the goals of assessment (i.e., improvement of service-learning experiences) are highlighted below. First, they may be used to begin a dialogue among the different parties with regard to their roles and responsibilities in service-learning. We hope the SLC and these corresponding assessment instruments will be used to stimulate a campus-wide conversation about what a college or university must do to ensure that service-learning programs achieve the goals of the program. Discussion of the SLC at campus workshops on service-learning, and even across campuses, can help identify and overcome challenges and barriers to service-learning.

Second, we believe these instruments are valuable for an internal dialogue for each of the SLC sections: students, faculty, and administrators. By completing the questionnaire periodically throughout one's engagement in a service-learning project, students, faculty, and administrators can determine the extent to which they are fulfilling their obligations with regard to the project. This activity will promote self-awareness and indicate potential areas of improvement. In this way, the assessment can be viewed as a component of critical reflection and allow for future beneficial steps to be formulated and enacted at the individual, course, and institutional levels.

Third, this formative assessment of service-learning can become part of the college accreditation process. As construed here, it involves a wide range of campus constituents and takes a comprehensive approach to understanding a program that speaks to the core of the college mission. These elements lend themselves well to the criteria and expectations of most college and university accreditation bodies.

Finally, the results of this assessment can be used for evaluation purposes, whether for the evaluation of students, instructors, courses, or administrative support for service-learning. This endeavor should be undertaken with care, for often evaluation impedes open dialogue, critical self-reflection, and continued growth and improvement. As discussed previously, one must be careful, especially with regard to students, not to use adherence to a prescribed set of moral values as a measure of academic performance. Although compliance with the code does not fully do that, it could be construed in that way. Conversely, it is important to hold all those involved in service-learning to this code.

This chapter provides the fundamental elements of validating the SLC and assessing the service-learning process with regard to compliance to the SLC. We encourage readers to incorporate assessment into service-learning projects and to share those results with us.

Student Form

Person Completing Form (check one):
_____ Student
_____ Faculty
_____ Community Agency Representative
_____ Peer (another student)
_____ Administrator
_____ Other: _____

Instructions: Please rate the extent to which the student adhered to each of the following items during the course of completing all requirements of the service-learning project. If you are the student, answer with regard to the extent to which your behavior was consistent with each of these items. When completing this questionnaire, use the scale below. For each item, circle the number that best indicates your agreement with each of the following statements.

0	1	2	3	4	5
Not Able to Rate	Strongly Disagree	Disagree	Neither Agree nor Disagree	Agree	Strongly Agree

During the course of the service-learning project, the student:

1) behaved as a professional representative of the college or university at all times.

   0   1   2   3   4   5

2) understood his or her role and its limitations in the context of the service-learning assignment.

   0   1   2   3   4   5

3) adhered to the policies and procedures of the community agency.

   0   1   2   3   4   5

4) treated service recipients in a manner consistent with ethical principles.

   0   1   2   3   4   5

0	1	2	3	4	5
Not Able to Rate	Strongly Disagree	Disagree	Neither Agree nor Disagree	Agree	Strongly Agree

5) fulfilled his or her service-learning commitment to the agency in accordance with the course requirements.

    0   1   2   3   4   5

6) abided by all applicable legal and ethical guidelines.

    0   1   2   3   4   5

7) recognized and reflected upon potential challenges to his or her personal value system.

    0   1   2   3   4   5

8) carefully considered all aspects of the service-learning assignment and consulted with faculty members if participation caused undue distress due to personal circumstances.

    0   1   2   3   4   5

Faculty Form

Person Completing Form (check one):
_____ Faculty
_____ Student
_____ Community Agency Representative
_____ Peer (another faculty member)
_____ Administrator
_____ Other: _____

Instructions: Please rate the extent to which the instructor adhered to each of the following items during the course of completing all requirements of the service-learning project. If you are the instructor, answer with regard to the extent to which your behavior was consistent with each of these items. When completing this questionnaire, use the scale below. For each item, circle the number that best indicates your agreement with each of the following statements.

0	1	2	3	4	5
Not Able to Rate	Strongly Disagree	Disagree	Neither Agree nor Disagree	Agree	Strongly Agree

During the course of the service-learning project, the instructor:

1) matched community needs with academic service-learning goals before the beginning of the project to ensure that academic and community service goals could be achieved.

   0   1   2   3   4   5

2) minimized potential harm to agencies, their constituents, and students.

   0   1   2   3   4   5

3) provided community agencies with a plan that included information about what was expected and required of students and the agency (e.g., accountability, commitment, consistency, and communication).

   0   1   2   3   4   5

0	1	2	3	4	5
Not Able to Rate	Strongly Disagree	Disagree	Neither Agree nor Disagree	Agree	Strongly Agree

4) developed course goals consistent with service-learning objectives and communicated to the students, both verbally and in writing, the parameters of the service-learning requirement, including:

a. academic objectives for the service-learning experience.

   0   1   2   3   4   5

b. community benefits.

   0   1   2   3   4   5

c. time requirements.

   0   1   2   3   4   5

d. student roles and responsibilities,

   0   1   2   3   4   5

e. legal and ethical guidelines on issues such as professionalism, liability, confidentiality, and insurance.

   0   1   2   3   4   5

f. responses to emergencies (e.g., threats, weather, health risks).

   0   1   2   3   4   5

g. expectations for integration into course material and reflection.

   0   1   2   3   4   5

h. alternative assignment unless college policy requires service-learning.

   0   1   2   3   4   5

5) trained and informed students of their responsibilities and the potential risks prior to the beginning of the service-learning activity.

   0   1   2   3   4   5

0	1	2	3	4	5
Not Able to Rate	Strongly Disagree	Disagree	Neither Agree nor Disagree	Agree	Strongly Agree

6) ensured that students understood the diverse characteristics of those with whom they worked.

    0   1   2   3   4   5

7) treated all students in a manner consistent with ethical principles.

    0   1   2   3   4   5

8) maintained involvement with community agencies throughout the process and responded to changing needs and circumstances.

    0   1   2   3   4   5

9) was available to students for consultation or referral for problem solving and conflict resolution.

    0   1   2   3   4   5

10) assessed the outcomes of this activity for the recipients, the community, and students.

    0   1   2   3   4   5

Administrator Form

Person Completing Form (check one):

_____ Administrator

_____ Faculty

_____ Student

_____ Community Agency Representative

_____ Peer (another administrator)

_____ Other: _____

Instructions: Please rate the extent to which the administrator adhered to each of the following items during the course of the service-learning project. If you are the administrator, answer with regard to the extent to which your behavior was consistent with each of these items. When completing this questionnaire, use the scale below. For each item, circle the number that best indicates your agreement with each of the following statements.

0	1	2	3	4	5
Not Able to Rate	Strongly Disagree	Disagree	Neither Agree nor Disagree	Agree	Strongly Agree

During the course of the service-learning project, the administrator:

1) recognized and supported opportunities for service-learning as part of a liberal education.

   0　　　　1　　　　2　　　　3　　　　4　　　　5

2) provided mechanisms for the institutionalization of civic engagement and resources for service-learning participation and service-related research.

   0　　　　1　　　　2　　　　3　　　　4　　　　5

3) was sensitive to and knowledgeable about community needs.

   0　　　　1　　　　2　　　　3　　　　4　　　　5

4) made every effort to minimize risky and unsafe locations and circumstances.

   0　　　　1　　　　2　　　　3　　　　4　　　　5

0	1	2	3	4	5
Not Able to Rate	Strongly Disagree	Disagree	Neither Agree nor Disagree	Agree	Strongly Agree

5) provided clear guidelines to faculty and students regarding liability and ethical issues.

   0   1   2   3   4   5

6) provided faculty with opportunities for training and education in service-learning curriculum infusion.

   0   1   2   3   4   5

7) treated all constituents in a manner consistent with ethical principles.

   0   1   2   3   4   5

Chapter Twenty

Service-Learning and Risk Management

Service-learning involves risk. To minimize risk in service-learning placements, faculty, students, and administrators must be prepared. Although extensive information has been published on the topic of risk management in service-learning (e.g., at www.servicelearning.org and www.compact.org), this chapter recommends risk management strategies that facilitate putting the SLC into practice. This chapter is not a legal document and should not take the place of legal advice or consultation, but rather highlights important steps to help professionals involved in service-learning minimize risk, especially for those who do not have extensive service-learning resources at their educational institutions.

Sources for Risk Management Information

There are several excellent sources of information regarding risk management, including the National Communication Association (www.natcom.org) and the National Service-Learning Clearinghouse (www.servicelearning.org). First and foremost, every institution should have a risk management plan, and service-learning practitioners must be aware that the contents of the plan are essential. If a plan is not available, each institution should create one for the protection of all involved parties. As stated in SLC III.4 and SLC III.5, *administrators shall make every effort to eliminate risky and unsafe locations and circumstances* and *provide clear guidelines to faculty and students regarding liability and ethical issues.* Creating an institutional risk management plan is one way to abide by this section of the SLC.

In the absence of a risk management plan, colleges and universities with established service-learning programs—for example, Brigham Young University–Idaho (BYU–Idaho), California State University (CSU), and Indiana University—are excellent sources of information on risk management. The partnering community agencies are another source of information on risk management. Nonprofit Risk Management (www.nonprofitrisk.org) and the Federal Volunteer Protection Act (VPA) of 1997 (42 U.S.C. 14501-05) also provide a wealth of information pertinent to service-learning. It is essential to consult individual state laws as well.

Steps in Risk Management

Risk management involves several steps:

1) Planning to minimize potential risks

2) Meeting with all parties to determine roles and responsibilities, and creating forms that clarify those agreements

3) Orientation and training for students involved in the service-learning project to emphasize the prevention aspect of the plan

4) Supervision

5) Evaluation of the process to identify risks and how to manage them

Planning

Planning is probably the most important and time-consuming part of the service-learning process (SLC II.1). When a problem occurs, a clear plan highlighting the risks and their management will indemnify the parties involved. The planning should start with the identification of any previous agreement made between the educational institution and the community agency of interest (National Service-Learning Clearinghouse Library, 2003). If an agreement already exists, it should be determined whether to keep the conditions of the existing agreement for the new service-learning placement, or to create a new agreement.

The next step in the planning process should be a visit to the community agency (CSU, 2004; National Service-Learning Clearinghouse Library, 2003). During the visit, the details of the service-learning experience—characteristics of the agency and its service, the nature of the service-learning experience, logistics, and risk identification (SLC II.1)—should be discussed at length. The visit should also include a tour of the community agency to determine any risk for the students, the agency, or the institution.

Agreements

The faculty and or program coordinator should prepare an agreement (BYU–Idaho, 2004; CSU, 2004; National Service-Learning Clearinghouse Library, 2003) that includes the information discussed with the community agency representatives, as well as risk management information (SLC II. 3). The agreement should then be approved by the educational institution and signed by a representative of the community agency. The agreement should specify the commitment to the service-learning experience from the perspectives of the educational institution and the community agency. It should include detailed information about the activities necessary to meet the goals of the experience, relevant policies and procedures of the agency and the institution, length of the experience and structure and support—supervision, training and orientation, work space, evaluation.

In addition to the syllabus, which includes information about the service-learning experience, the faculty should further prepare an additional written agreement, similar to an informed consent form, for the students (BYU Idaho, 2004; CSU, 2004; National Service-Learning Clearinghouse Library, 2003) as proposed in SLC II.4. The agreement should include essential information regarding expectations and limitations of the service-learning experiences (CSU, 2004; National Service-Learning Clearinghouse Library, 2003). The faculty should discuss the agreement with the students and have them sign it. This discussion will help ensure that students are aware of the risks associated with the service-learning experience. Faculty should also make sure that the site supervisor reviews and signs the agreement. Finally, the faculty should sign it and retain a copy. By including specific behaviors in the agreement, students will better understand their obligation to *behave as professional representatives of the college/university at all times* (SLC I.1).

Additional Forms

Depending on the educational institution, community agency, and state and federal regulations, additional forms may also be required. For instance, many educational institutions require students to sign a *release form* or *waiver* when participating in off-campus activities (National Service-Learning Clearinghouse Library, 2003). Faculty should be aware that there are insurance policies for professional coverage that are available for specific students and programs.

Another set of forms, based on state and federal regulations regarding fingerprints and criminal background checks, may be required for students whose service-learning placements are in agencies with protected populations (CSU, 2004). The fees for the background check are usually not covered by the agency. Some background check processes may take a long period of time, so faculty should be prepared well in advance. Fingerprint legislation is very clear regarding personal privacy. Since the community agency is requiring the fingerprint, only the community agency will receive the results. This will have an impact on students who take more than one service-learning course that requires fingerprinting.

It is also best practice to use time sheets (CSU, 2004; National Service-Learning Clearinghouse Library, 2003). There are several options, but three time sheets are essential (CSU, 2004). The first form is the community agency sign-in sheet. This is the form located at the community agency for each course involved in a service-learning experience at the site. The form should include the names of the students, sign-in time, sign-out time, activity, and supervisor signature.

The second time sheet form is the faculty record of the service-learning placement. This form should contain a list of the students, placements, and times.

The form is completed after the students return their agreements to the faculty. The third form is the student's own time sheet. This form is to be filled out by the students every time they go to the service-learning placement. The form should be signed by the site supervisor as an additional verification of the hours the student served at the site. The faculty should collect or review the forms at least twice during the placement, to ensure the student is on track to fulfill the requirements and to check for the activities performed at the placement.

These three forms can be used as a cross-reference in case an accident or claim is brought up against any of the parties (CSU, 2004). The forms should be stored at a central location for at least a year (the typical statute of limitation in this kind of claim), after which they can be discarded. In the event that students are injured at the site, they must be able to prove that they were at the agency when the injury occurred. This is required by law in order to receive compensation. These forms can be useful in support of such a claim.

Orientation

Before students begin the service-learning experience, they should participate in an orientation process (SLC II.5). Best practice recommendations suggest two orientations (BYU–Idaho, 2004; CSU, 2004). The first one should be on campus and cover information regarding the work to be done by the students, how they should conduct themselves when working in the community, and risk management (SLC I.1–8). This orientation should be based on the information shared between the educational institution and the community agency. At the first orientation, the student agreement and any other forms should be distributed and discussed.

From a risk management perspective, special emphasis should be placed on orientation and training regarding safety procedures, potential dangers, and risk management from the institution and community agency perspectives. A list of guidelines and limitations should also be provided to students (SLC I.1–6).

The second orientation should occur at the site of the service-learning placement and should address emergency policies and procedures, as well as rules and regulations of the placement. Both orientations should be mandatory for all students before the beginning of the service-learning placement. By the end of the orientations, the students should have their questions answered and should have signed the student agreement that ensures they understand the nature of the service-learning placement and agree to the terms.

Supervision

Having adequate supervision on site and in the classroom (SLC II.9) creates a safer environment for all the parties involved in the service-learning experience (BYU–Idaho, 2004; CSU, 2004; National Service-

Learning Clearinghouse Library, 2003). To successfully supervise, one has to clearly understand the nature of the placement as well as risk management and liability issues. A component of the faculty supervision includes involvement with the community agency throughout the whole process and faculty participation in the service-learning activity (SLC II.8). We recommend faculty visits and participation while the students are present to gain first-hand knowledge of the situations that students are experiencing.

Open, frequent, and clear communication is very important in the risk management plan (SLC II.2). Students and supervisors should know whom to contact in case a question or emergency arises during the service-learning experience. Frequent communication between the supervisors and the students will allow them to identify any issues or concerns and address them early in the process (National Service-Learning Clearinghouse Library, 2003).

Evaluation

An essential aspect of the risk management process is evaluation (SLC II.10). Starting with the initial visit with the community agency representatives, evaluations should be discussed (CSU, 2004). The timelines of the evaluations should be specified in the agreement with the community partner and in the student agreement. Evaluations from all the parties involved will be a useful way for the educational institution to determine the value of the service-learning experience. When the evaluations are collected and processed, the faculty or the educational institution should determine whether to renew the agreement with the community agency. For suggestions regarding evaluation of the implementation of the SLC, see Chapter 19.

A final visit is recommended during which the faculty and program coordinators assess the outcomes of the service-learning activities for the recipients, the community, and the students. Faculty should meet with the community agency to discuss the service-learning experience, especially from risk management and liability standpoints. What should be done differently next time?

Other Issues

Transportation

Educational institutions usually state clearly in waivers or informed consents that they are not liable for transporting students to and from community agency sites (Cedar Crest College, 2002; CSU, 2004; National Service-Learning Clearinghouse Library, 2003). When transport vehicles belong to the educational institution or are driven by one of its representatives, adherence to best practices will help minimize the risks to students and drivers. For instance, drivers should be screened and trained, they should follow safety precautions, and the vehicles should be safe and kept to an appropriate maintenance schedule.

Faculty should determine the risks when public transportation is used and take actions to minimize risks (e.g., pairing students who travel to the site by bus). Liability is greatly reduced when students are responsible for their own transportation to and from the service-learning site.

Service-Learning File

A service-learning reporting file (National Service-Learning Clearinghouse Library, 2003) should be kept and should include incidents, safety violations, time sheets, and record of orientations. The file should be used as a source of information in the planning of future projects to help prevent the recurrence of any adverse situations.

International Service-Learning Experience

International service-learning experiences have to be considered as special circumstances. Many of the guidelines discussed above apply to this situation; however, they have to be adapted for the country where the placement will take place. Other issues must be considered, such as the requirements to enter the country, customs and local information regarding the placement, information regarding the U.S. embassy in the country, and means of communication.

Insurance

Students should be made aware of the types of insurance available to them or necessary for placement in service-learning. Insurance is available to students through different professional associations. State legislation may require that the educational institution insure the student when service-learning is a mandatory component of the school curriculum.

Conclusion

Risk management is an ongoing process. Before the beginning of each service-learning experience, the educational institution, in conjunction with the community partner, should prepare a plan to minimize potential risks for all parties. In the event of an accident, all parties involved are candidates for financial responsibility. Even though the faculty can be named in lawsuits, they may be indemnified and/or protected by the institution as long as they were acting within the scope of their work. The students may also be protected if they were following the plan delineated at the beginning of the placement, as described in the agreements, and as long as they were acting within the scope of their duties and responsibilities without malicious intent.

The presentation of the information to the students should not scare them, but should instead prepare them for real-world situations they will encounter. If all parties are "adequately informed and oriented, the risk management process will only serve to strengthen community-campus partnerships by furthering mutual trust and understanding" (National Service-Learning Clearinghouse Library, 2003).

Community Partner Agreement

General Guidelines

1) Identify the educational institution and community partner entering into agreement.

2) List general considerations, including:

   • Participants in the service-learning experience

   • Time of beginning and end of service-learning experience

   • Termination of the service-learning experience

   • The renewal process

3) Describe the program/activities for the service-learning placement.

4) Describe the educational institution and its representatives' roles and responsibilities, especially:

   • Preparation of agreements

   • Orientation

   • Supervision

   • Reflection

   • Evaluation

5) Describe the students' roles and responsibilities in the service-learning placement.

6) Describe the community partner's roles and responsibilities, such as:

   • Tour of site

   • Orientation

   • Training

   • Supervision

   • Evaluation

7) Collect signatures of representatives from the educational institution and community partner.

Student Agreement

Student Information

Name: ID:

Address:

Phone #:   E-mail address:

Contact person in case of emergency: Relationship:

Phone # (daytime):   Phone # (evenings):

Service-Learning Course Information

Course Name/Number: Semester/Quarter:

Course instructor:

Phone #:   E-mail address:

Best time to be reached:

Service-Learning Placement Information

Agency name/site: Phone #:

Supervisor name: Phone #:

Address:

Position title:

Total number of hours: Beginning date: End date:

Time assigned at placement:

Learning objectives

Service objectives

Site supervisor's responsibilities

Site supervisor's signature

Faculty approval of plan and signature

List of do's and don'ts for the students

Student agreement and signature

Student Time Sheet

Student name:

Course:

Semester/Quarter:

Service-learning placement:

Date	Time in	Time out	Total hours	Total hours to date	Supervisor's initials

Comments:

Supervisor's signature:

Student's signature:

Date:

Appendix

Additional Dilemmas

This appendix contains several scenarios similar to those discussed in the preceding chapters. These dilemmas can be used to facilitate discussion. By assuming the role of a student, faculty member, or administrator, the reader can participate in multiple perspectives. Reflective questions follow each scenario. These questions are based on the model of ethical decision-making and are designed to help the reader work through the model to come to a possible resolution of the dilemma. This process affords the opportunity to engage in values clarification and critical thinking through discussion of the issues, problems, and dilemmas associated with service-learning experiences.

1) Identify the ethical dilemma.

2) Why is it an ethical dilemma? Identify the relevant section(s) (i.e., students, faculty, and administrators) and the specific codes (e.g., SLC II.1).

3) Identify and list information you think would be helpful in making a decision.

4) List at least three possible solutions to this dilemma.

5) Which of the proposed solutions would you choose?

6) Why would you choose this solution?

7) How would you evaluate whether this is a good solution?

Exercise 1

A number of social work students are taking a full credit load of classes for the semester. One of the social work classes includes a service-learning component. The students receive the service-learning assignments midway through the semester. Several students realize that the assignment conflicts with other classes they are taking. They tell their social work professor that in order to complete this requirement, they would miss three to five classes in their other courses. They also explain that their other professors have attendance policies such that these absences would affect their grades. The social work professor tells the students that they must participate in the service-learning assignment, otherwise they will not fulfill the social work course requirement.

If there is an ethical dilemma, answer the following seven questions:

1) Identify the ethical dilemma.

2) Why is it an ethical dilemma? Identify the relevant section(s) (i.e., students, faculty, and administrators) and the specific codes (e.g., SLC II.1).

3) Identify and list information you think would be helpful in making a decision.

4) List at least three possible solutions to this dilemma.

5) Which of the proposed solutions would you choose?

6) Why would you choose this solution?

7) How would you evaluate whether this is a good solution?

Exercise 2

A nonprofit agency has been asked to upgrade its outcomes evaluation. One of the board members, a faculty member at the local college, contacts a colleague who teaches a research course to find out if she would be interested in integrating a project into her class. A meeting is set up between the professor and the agency director. The guidelines for the project are established. The students meet with the agency director to learn about the program, and they discuss different possibilities for the outcomes evaluation. Midyear, the professor decides to take another teaching position at a different institution. The students have already begun the project, but they are not close to finishing it. The board of the nonprofit agency is upset with the faculty member and the institution for failing to complete this project. The board asks the president of the college to remedy the situation.

If there is an ethical dilemma, answer the following seven questions:

1) Identify the ethical dilemma.

2) Why is it an ethical dilemma? Identify the relevant section(s) (i.e., students, faculty, and administrators) and the specific codes (e.g., SLC II.1).

3) Identify and list information you think would be helpful in making a decision.

4) List at least three possible solutions to this dilemma.

5) Which of the proposed solutions would you choose?

6) Why would you choose this solution?

7) How would you evaluate whether this is a good solution?

Exercise 3

A course titled "Medical Ethics" has a service-learning component in which students spend time with patients at a local AIDS hospice. During their time at the hospice, the students converse with the patients, play games with them, and help the staff meet the patients' needs. The students subsequently reflect on their service-learning experiences in journals and then write a paper applying their experiences to the course material. Jorge, one of the students in the class, is strongly homophobic and, based on his religious views, believes homosexuality is morally wrong. He refuses to participate in the service-learning experience.

If there is an ethical dilemma, answer the following seven questions:

1) Identify the ethical dilemma.

2) Why is it an ethical dilemma? Identify the relevant section(s) (i.e., students, faculty, and administrators) and the specific codes (e.g., SLC II.1).

3) Identify and list information you think would be helpful in making a decision.

4) List at least three possible solutions to this dilemma.

5) Which of the proposed solutions would you choose?

6) Why would you choose this solution?

7) How would you evaluate whether this is a good solution?

Exercise 4

Dr. Smith is teaching a business course titled "Organizational Ethics" that includes a service-learning project in the course syllabus. Students taking this course are required to spend 20 hours during the semester interviewing migrant workers at a local mushroom farm to understand their working conditions. Dr. Smith's academic goals include having students develop an understanding of ethical issues related to corporate social responsibility. He believes that weekly contact with the migrant workers will raise his students' awareness of these issues. One student, Sam, says that migrant workers should not be permitted to work in the United States because they take jobs from American workers. For this reason, he refuses to participate in the service-learning project. He accuses Dr. Smith of having a social agenda and of trying to influence Sam's value system, instead of teaching Sam the content of corporate ethics. Dr. Smith takes the position that he is the instructor of the course and can therefore develop course requirements that address the academic goals of the course.

If there is an ethical dilemma, answer the following seven questions:

1) Identify the ethical dilemma.

2) Why is it an ethical dilemma? Identify the relevant section(s) (i.e., students, faculty, and administrators) and the specific codes (e.g., SLC II.1).

3) Identify and list information you think would be helpful in making a decision.

4) List at least three possible solutions to this dilemma.

5) Which of the proposed solutions would you choose?

6) Why would you choose this solution?

7) How would you evaluate whether this is a good solution?

Exercise 5

The professor of a course with a service-learning component routinely has students discuss their experiences in class as part of the reflection component of the course. In the process of this discussion, a student reveals that a client at a community agency has been involved in a complicated legal battle for custody of his children. The student is quite explicit about the unusual circumstances of this case. After class, another student reveals to the professor that she was very upset by the class discussion, because the client is her cousin.

If there is an ethical dilemma, answer the following seven questions:

1) Identify the ethical dilemma.

2) Why is it an ethical dilemma? Identify the relevant section(s) (i.e., students, faculty, and administrators) and the specific codes (e.g., SLC II.1).

3) Identify and list information you think would be helpful in making a decision.

4) List at least three possible solutions to this dilemma.

5) Which of the proposed solutions would you choose?

6) Why would you choose this solution?

7) How would you evaluate whether this is a good solution?

Exercise 6

Sam, a chemistry major, is working on a service-learning research project that involves testing the soil in a neighborhood located near a landfill that has been cited many times for noncompliance with Environmental Protection Agency standards. The results of the project will be shared with local municipal authorities who are interested in data related to soil contaminants. Sam discovers that there are dangerous levels of toxins in the soil of two families who have young children. Sam wonders whether he should share this information with the families.

If there is an ethical dilemma, answer the following seven questions:

1) Identify the ethical dilemma.

2) Why is it an ethical dilemma? Identify the relevant section(s) (i.e., students, faculty, and administrators) and the specific codes (e.g., SLC II.1).

3) Identify and list information you think would be helpful in making a decision.

4) List at least three possible solutions to this dilemma.

5) Which of the proposed solutions would you choose?

6) Why would you choose this solution?

7) How would you evaluate whether this is a good solution?

Exercise 7

Leo is working at a center that provides telephone support for children. The mission of the center clearly states that all calls are confidential and anonymous. The callers are asked not to provide their names or any identifying information. The children are encouraged to call the center if they are home alone after school, have a problem they cannot discuss with anyone else, or need information about where to get some help. Leo receives a call from a child who does not give his name, but tells Leo a story about a situation with which Leo is personally familiar. From the circumstances the child describes, Leo knows the identity of the caller. From the information the child has told him, he also knows that the child's father is engaging in illegal activities. Leo considers his ethical responsibilities in this situation.

If there is an ethical dilemma, answer the following seven questions:

1) Identify the ethical dilemma.

2) Why is it an ethical dilemma? Identify the relevant section(s) (i.e., students, faculty, and administrators) and the specific codes (e.g., SLC II.1).

3) Identify and list information you think would be helpful in making a decision.

4) List at least three possible solutions to this dilemma.

5) Which of the proposed solutions would you choose?

6) Why would you choose this solution?

7) How would you evaluate whether this is a good solution?

Exercise 8

In the spring semester, a service-learning coordinator at a large public university procures a van to transport students to and from service-learning placements. This plan was approved by the service-learning coordinator's immediate supervisor, the assistant dean of academic affairs. The following summer, the service-learning coordinator resigns from the position. The assistant academic dean hires a new service-learning coordinator. The new coordinator places the van in service in the beginning of the fall semester, following the plan the previous coordinator had set up.

Approximately four weeks into the semester, the use of the van comes to the attention of the vice president for finance. This person was not consulted by the assistant dean before the dean approved this plan. The vice president informs the assistant dean that the van cannot be used for this purpose, due to liability concerns. Approximately 100 students at a dozen community sites are currently using the van. Loss of this transportation service will make it extremely difficult for the students to complete their service-learning assignments.

If there is an ethical dilemma, answer the following seven questions:

1) Identify the ethical dilemma.

2) Why is it an ethical dilemma? Identify the relevant section(s) (i.e., students, faculty, and administrators) and the specific codes (e.g., SLC II.1).

3) Identify and list information you think would be helpful in making a decision.

4) List at least three possible solutions to this dilemma.

5) Which of the proposed solutions would you choose?

6) Why would you choose this solution?

7) How would you evaluate whether this is a good solution?

Exercise 9

As part of the strategic visioning process, a moderately sized public institution identifies its commitment to public engagement in the form of internships, community service, and service-learning experiences. Because of this mandate, several faculty members request professional development training funds for the infusion of service-learning into the curriculum. They first contact their department chairpersons, who refer them to the deans of their respective colleges. The deans believe that allocating these funds is the responsibility of the provost. However, the provost believes that faculty can engage in self-training and acquire the needed skills on their own. She is unwilling to divert money from a limited professional development fund to those who desire training on service-learning. The provost's rationale is that sufficient guidelines and needed information would be provided by the reading of service-learning texts and research on the Internet for service-learning models at other institutions.

If there is an ethical dilemma, answer the following seven questions:

1) Identify the ethical dilemma.

2) Why is it an ethical dilemma? Identify the relevant section(s) (i.e., students, faculty, and administrators) and the specific codes (e.g., SLC II.1).

3) Identify and list information you think would be helpful in making a decision.

4) List at least three possible solutions to this dilemma.

5) Which of the proposed solutions would you choose?

6) Why would you choose this solution?

7) How would you evaluate whether this is a good solution?

Exercise 10

Students in a conflict resolution class meet once a week with inmates of a small local county jail. This service-learning requirement involves several different activities, including engaging in conversation, playing cards, and helping prisoners read or write letters. During class discussion, several students remark that they feel uncomfortable about the attitudes of the male correctional officers in the facility. The students report being told, "Inmates are just that, inmates. They are a low form of the human race. Because they are in jail, they deserve no respect, consideration, or privileges, and they certainly do not deserve a second chance." Not only do the guards use disrespectful and harsh language toward the prisoners, but they also talk about the student service-learners. Several students overhear the guards calling them "bleeding hearts" who have no place in a correctional facility because they are too soft. After only three weeks, these students are unsure about fulfilling their service-learning commitment and plan to report their observations and experiences to the warden.

If there is an ethical dilemma, answer the following seven questions:

1) Identify the ethical dilemma.

2) Why is it an ethical dilemma? Identify the relevant section(s) (i.e., students, faculty, and administrators) and the specific codes (e.g., SLC II.1).

3) Identify and list information you think would be helpful in making a decision.

4) List at least three possible solutions to this dilemma.

5) Which of the proposed solutions would you choose?

6) Why would you choose this solution?

7) How would you evaluate whether this is a good solution?

Exercise 11

The service-learning requirement for students in a selected topics class in sociology is to provide companionship to residents at a local nursing home. Malik, a senior sociology major, explains to the class that she is expected to play games and read to those residents who refuse to leave their rooms. In some cases, she will be given hand lotion to rub residents' hands. After two visits, she feels depressed and uncomfortable. She says, "the frustrating thing was that these people did not really need or want a stranger bothering them. These were people who wanted to be left alone. The girl in charge of volunteering had told me that they had pretty much been loners or quiet for most of their lives. She said that they still wanted them to be somewhat social, but I didn't think it was the best thing to do." Malik believes that if the residents want to be alone, it makes them uncomfortable to have a stranger in their bedrooms trying to talk to them. She says she does not know these people and has never had the experience of visiting people alone whom she had never met. In addition, Malik is concerned about forcing people to engage in activities that make them feel uncomfortable.

If there is an ethical dilemma, answer the following seven questions:

1) Identify the ethical dilemma.

2) Why is it an ethical dilemma? Identify the relevant section(s) (i.e., students, faculty, and administrators) and the specific codes (e.g., SLC II.1).

3) Identify and list information you think would be helpful in making a decision.

4) List at least three possible solutions to this dilemma.

5) Which of the proposed solutions would you choose?

6) Why would you choose this solution?

7) How would you evaluate whether this is a good solution?

Exercise 12

Shayla, an occupational therapy assistant student at a small religious college, is involved in service-learning activities at a local rehabilitation facility. She has developed effective professional relationships with several staff members and enjoys working with the patients. However, Shayla notices on two occasions that patients are left alone, strapped in their chairs for long periods of time. She believes this is inhumane and unjust. The next time Shayla sees this, she decides to remove a patient's straps to make him more comfortable. Later that afternoon, the floor supervisor at the facility calls the department chair of occupational therapy at the college. She reports Shayla's "unprofessional behavior," and requests that Shayla be removed from the service-learning site.

If there is an ethical dilemma, answer the following seven questions:

1) Identify the ethical dilemma.

2) Why is it an ethical dilemma? Identify the relevant section(s) (i.e., students, faculty, and administrators) and the specific codes (e.g., SLC II.1).

3) Identify and list information you think would be helpful in making a decision.

4) List at least three possible solutions to this dilemma.

5) Which of the proposed solutions would you choose?

6) Why would you choose this solution?

7) How would you evaluate whether this is a good solution?

Exercise 13

Taking advantage of a presidential election year, Dr. Rodriguez incorporates a service-learning component into his American government class. He believes that whatever the political party affiliation of his students, they will benefit from volunteering during the on-campus visit of one of the candidates. Jameda, one of Dr. Rodriguez's students, believes this candidate is "unsympathetic and unsupportive of the needs of her people."

Therefore, she refuses to engage in this activity and requests that she be excused from this requirement.

If there is an ethical dilemma, answer the following seven questions:

1) Identify the ethical dilemma.

2) Why is it an ethical dilemma? Identify the relevant section(s) (i.e., students, faculty, and administrators) and the specific codes (e.g., SLC II.1).

3) Identify and list information you think would be helpful in making a decision.

4) List at least three possible solutions to this dilemma.

5) Which of the proposed solutions would you choose?

6) Why would you choose this solution?

7) How would you evaluate whether this is a good solution?

Exercise 14

In a management of offenders class, upper-level criminal justice majors are expected to engage in a service-learning project with a juvenile probation agency. Students work with first-time offenders under the supervision of several probation officers. Activities include answering pagers, performing curfew visitations, collecting drug tests, and conducting counseling visitations. Tonya, one of the students in the class, views this as an opportunity to work in a multiracial environment. She is disappointed to find, though, that when staff members speak to colleagues in the presence of offenders, they only speak Spanish. She feels excluded and later becomes upset when she realizes that offenders have noticed this behavior as well. In particular, one says, "Here we go again. I can never understand what you guys are talking about!" Tonya questions the cultural sensitivity of those who are working with young people in such a diverse community and considers bringing this to the director's attention.

If there is an ethical dilemma, answer the following seven questions:

1) Identify the ethical dilemma.

2) Why is it an ethical dilemma? Identify the relevant section(s) (i.e., students, faculty, and administrators) and the specific codes (e.g., SLC II.1).

3) Identify and list information you think would be helpful in making a decision.

4) List at least three possible solutions to this dilemma.

5) Which of the proposed solutions would you choose?

6) Why would you choose this solution?

7) How would you evaluate whether this is a good solution?

Exercise 15

As part of the course requirements for a lifespan development class, students are engaged in a service-learning activity at a local soup kitchen, where more than 75 meals are served each day. When the director of public relations at the college learns about this, she sends a camera and video crew to record the community involvement of these students. The director of the soup kitchen becomes extremely upset, informing the camera crew that their presence could deter clients from coming for their only meal of the day. Students discuss the impact of this incident on the clients, the community, the college, and themselves.

If there is an ethical dilemma, answer the following seven questions:

1) Identify the ethical dilemma.

2) Why is it an ethical dilemma? Identify the relevant section(s) (i.e., students, faculty, and administrators) and the specific codes (e.g., SLC II.1).

3) Identify and list information you think would be helpful in making a decision.

4) List at least three possible solutions to this dilemma.

5) Which of the proposed solutions would you choose?

6) Why would you choose this solution?

7) How would you evaluate whether this is a good solution?

Bibliography

American Association of University Professors. (1990). *Policy documents and reports.* Washington, DC: Author.

American Council on Education. (1995–2005). *Strategic priorities: Our plan of action.* Retrieved January 14, 2005, from http://www .acenet.edu/plan/strategic-priorities.cfm

American Counseling Association. (1995). *Code of ethics.* Retrieved December 14, 2004, from http://www.counseling.org/Content/ NavigationMenu/RESOURCES/ETHICS/ACA_Code_of_Ethics.htm

American Medical Association. (2001). *Principles of medical ethics.* Retrieved January 14, 2005, from http://www.ama-assn.org/ama/ pub/category/2512.html

American Society for Public Administration. (2000). *ASPA's code of ethics.* Retrieved December 17, 2004, from http://www.aspanet.org/script content/index_codeofethics.cfm

American Society of Civil Engineers. (1996). *Code of ethics.* Retrieved December 14, 2004, from http://www.asce.org/inside/codeofethics.cfm

Association for Computing Machinery. (1997). *ACM code of ethics and professional conduct.* Retrieved December 17, 2004, from http:// www.acm.org/constitution/code.html

Astin, A. W. (1991). *Assessment for excellence: The philosophy and practice of assessment and evaluation in higher education.* New York, NY: American Council on Education/Macmillan.

Astin, A. W., & Sax, L. J. (1998). How undergraduates are affected by service participation. *Journal of College Student Development, 39*(3), 251–263.

Astin, A. W., Sax, L. J., & Avalos, J. (1999). Long-term effects of volunteerism during the undergraduate years. *Review of Higher Education, 21*(2), 187–202.

Astin, A. W., Vogelgesang, L. J., Ikeda, E. K., & Yee, J. A. (2000). *How service learning affects students.* Los Angeles, CA: University of California, Higher Education Research Institute.

Barber, B. R. (2000). *A passion for democracy: American essays.* Princeton, NJ: Princeton University Press.

Batchelder, T. H., & Root, S. (1994). Effects of an undergraduate program to integrate academic learning and service: Cognitive, prosocial cognitive, and identity outcomes. *Journal of Adolescence, 17,* 341–355.

Bentham, J. (1939). An introduction to the principles of morals and legislation. In E. A. Burtt (Ed.), *The English philosophers from Bacon to Mill* (pp. 792–856). New York, NY: Random House. (Original work published 1789)

Boatright, J. R. (2000). *Ethics and the conduct of business.* Upper Saddle River, NJ: Prentice Hall.

Boss, J. A. (1994). The effect of community service work on the moral development of college ethics students. *Journal of Moral Education, 23*(2), 183–197.

Boud, D. (1990). Assessment and the promotion of academic values. *Studies in Higher Education, 15*(1), 101–111.

Boyle-Baise, M., & Kilbane, J. (2000, Fall). What really happens? A look inside service-learning for multicultural teacher education. *Michigan Journal of Service Learning, 7,* 54–64.

Brigham Young University–Idaho. (2004). *Liability concerns and risk management.* Retrieved June 8, 2004, from http://byui.edu/Service Learning/subpages/fgliability.htm

Bringle, R. G., & Duffy, D. K. (Eds.). (1998). *With service in mind: Concepts and models for service-learning in psychology.* Washington, DC: American Association for Higher Education.

Bringle, R. G., & Hatcher, J. (1995). A service learning curriculum for faculty. *Michigan Journal of Community Service Learning, 2*(3), 112–122.

Bringle, R. G., & Hatcher, J. A. (2002). Campus-community partnerships: The terms of engagement. *Journal of Social Issues, 58*(3), 503–516.

Bringle, R. G., & Kremer, J. F. (1993). An evaluation of an intergenerational service-learning project for undergraduates. *Educational Gerontology, 19,* 407–416.

Bringle, R. G., Phillips, M. A., & Hudson, M. (2004). *The measure of service-learning: Research scales to assess student experiences.* Washington, DC: American Psychological Association.

California State University. (2004). *Community service learning in the CSU.* Retrieved December 14, 2004, from http://www.calstate.edu/CSL/

Callan, E. (1997). *Creating citizens: Political education and liberal democracy.* New York, NY: Oxford University Press.

Campus Compact. (1993). *Rethinking tradition: Integrating service with academic study on college campuses.* Denver, CO: Education Commission of the States

Campus Compact. (1999). *Presidents' declaration on the civic responsibility of higher education.* Retrieved December 14, 2004, from http://www.compact.org/presidential/declaration.html

Campus Compact. (2003). *2003 annual membership survey.* Retrieved December 14, 2004, from http://www.compact.org/newscc/stats2003/

Campus Compact. (2004). *Center for Liberal Education and Civic Engagement.* Retrieved December 14, 2004, from http://www.compact.org/civic/CLECE/principles

Cedar Crest College. (2002). *Lutz Center for Community Service.* Retrieved December 14, 2004, from http://www2.cedarcrest.edu/studentaffairs/commserv/index.html

Chambers, T., & Burkhardt, J. (2004). Fulfilling the promise of civic engagement. *Priorities, 22,* 1–15.

Chartered Financial Analyst. (1999). *Code of ethics and standards of practice.* Retrieved December 17, 2004, from http://www.cfainstitute.org/standards/pdf/CodeandStandards.pdf

Colby, A., Ehrlich, T., Beaumont, E., & Stephens, J. (2003). *Educating citizens: Preparing America's undergraduates for lives of moral and civic responsibility.* San Francisco, CA: Jossey-Bass.

Colby, A., Kohlberg, L., Speicher, B., Hewer, A., Candee, D., Gibbs, J. C., et al. (1987a). *The measurement of moral judgment: Vol. 1. Theoretical foundations and research validation.* New York, NY: Cambridge University Press.

Colby, A., Kohlberg, L., Speicher, B., Hewer, A., Candee, D., Gibbs, J. C., et al. (1987b). *The measurement of moral judgment: Vol. 2. Standard issue scoring manual.* New York, NY: Cambridge University Press.

Cook, K., Hillman, E., & Carmer, G. (June, 2003). *Service-learning projects as triggers for the development of moral empathy in Christian college students.* Paper presented at the Critical Issues Conference, Seattle, WA. Retrieved December 15, 2004, from www.cccu.org/docLib/20030903_CAP_Presentation.doc

Corey, G., Corey, M. S., & Callahan, P. (1998). *Issues and ethics in the helping professions* (5th ed.). Pacific Grove, CA: Brooks/Cole.

Corey, G., Corey, M. S., & Haynes, R. (1998). *Facilitator's resource manual for ethics in action* (Institutional version). Pacific Grove, CA: ITP.

Dewey, J. (1997). *Democracy and education: An introduction to the philosophy of education.* New York, NY: Free Press. (Original work published 1916)

Dunlap, M. R. (1998). Methods of supporting students' critical reflection in courses incorporating service-learning. *Teaching of Psychology, 25*(3), 208–210.

Dunlap, M. R. (2000). *Reaching out to children and families: Students model effective community service.* New York, NY: Rowman & Littlefield.

Ehrlich, T. (Ed.). (2000). *Civic responsibility and higher education.* Phoenix, AZ: American Council on Education/Oryx Press.

Ehrlich, T. (2003). The impact of higher education on moral and civic responsibility. *Journal of College and Character, 2.* Retrieved December 15, 2004, from http://collegevalues.org/articles.cfm?a=1&id=37

Eyler, J., & Giles, D. E., Jr. (1999). *Where's the learning in service-learning?* San Francisco, CA: Jossey-Bass.

Eyler, J. S., Giles, D. E., & Braxton, J. (1997). The impact of service-learning on college students. *Michigan Journal of Community Service Learning, 4,* 5–15.

Ferrari, J. R., & Jason, L. A. (1996). Integrating research and community service: Incorporating research skills into service-learning experiences. *College Student Journal, 30*(4), 444–451.

Fish, S. (2003, May 16). Aim low. *Chronicle of Higher Education,* p. C5.

Galston, W. (1991). *Liberal purposes: Good, virtues, and diversity in the liberal state.* Cambridge, England: Cambridge University Press.

Giles, D. E., & Eyler, J. S. (1994). The impact of a college community service laboratory on students' personal, social and cognitive outcomes. *Journal of Adolescence, 17,* 327–339.

Gilligan, C. (1982). *In a different voice: Psychological theory and women's development.* Cambridge, MA: Harvard University Press.

Gorman, M., Duffy, J., & Heffernan, M. (1994). Service experience and the moral development of college students. *Religious Education, 89*(3), 422–431.

Gredler, M. E. (1996). *Program evaluation.* Englewood Cliffs, NJ: Prentice Hall.

Honnet, E. P., & Poulson, S. J. (1989). *Principles of good practice for combining service and learning* (Wingspread special report). Racine, WI: The Johnson Foundation.

Howard, J. (1993). Community service-learning in the curriculum. In J. Howard (Ed.), *Praxis I: A faculty casebook on community service-learning* (pp. 3–11). Ann Arbor, MI: Office of Community Service-learning Press.

Jacoby, B. (1996). *Service-learning in higher education: Concepts and practices*. San Francisco, CA: Jossey-Bass.

Juhn, G., Tang, J., Piessens, P., Grant, U., Johnson, N., & Murray, H. (1999). Community learning: The reach for health nursing program–middle school collaboration. *Journal of Nursing Education, 38*(5), 215–221.

Kant, I. (1949). *Critique of practical reason and other writings in moral philosophy* (L. W. Beck, Ed. & Trans.). Chicago, IL: University of Chicago Press. (Original work published 1788)

Kaye, C. B. (2003). *The complete guide to service learning: Proven, practical ways to engage students in civic responsibility, academic curriculum, and social action*. Minneapolis, MN: Free Spirit.

Kearsley, G. (1994–2004). *Explorations in learning and instruction: The theory into practice database*. Retrieved December 15, 2004, from http://tip.psychology.org

Kendall, J. C. (1991). Combining service and learning: An introduction for cooperative education professionals. *Journal of Cooperative Education, 27*(2), 9–26.

Kendrick, J. R. (1996). Outcomes of service-learning in an introduction to sociology course. *Michigan Journal of Community Service-Learning, 3*, 72–81.

Kenny, M., Simon, L. A. K., Brabeck, K., & Lerner, R. M. (Eds.). (2002). *Learning to serve: Promoting civil society through service-learning* (Vol. 7). Norwell, MA: Kluwer.

Kohlberg, L. (1971). *The philosophy of moral education*. New York, NY: Harper & Row.

Kohlberg, L. (1981). *The philosophy of moral development: Moral stages and the idea of justice*. New York, NY: Harper & Row.

Kretchmar, M. D. (2001). Service-learning in a general psychology class: Description, preliminary evaluation, and recommendations. *Teaching of Psychology, 28*(1), 5–10.

Lazerson, M., Wagener, U., & Shumanis, N. (1999). *What makes a revolution: Teaching and learning in higher education, 1980–2000.* Stanford, CA: Stanford University, National Center for Postsecondary Improvement. Retrieved December 15, 2004, from http://www.stanford.edu/group/ncpi/documents/pdfs/5-11_revolution.pdf

Leming, J. S. (2001). Integrating a structured ethical reflection curriculum into high school community service experiences: Impact on students' sociomoral development. *Adolescence, 36*(141), 33–45.

Lisman, C. D. (1999). *Service-learning resource guide.* Washington, DC: American Association of Community Colleges.

Lissitz, R. W., & Schafer, W. D. (Eds.). (2002). *Assessment in educational reform: Both means and ends.* Boston, MA: Allyn & Bacon.

Lucas, C. J. (1994). *American higher education: A history.* New York, NY: St. Martin's Press.

Mallory, B. L., & Thomas, N. L. (2003, September/October). When the medium is the message: Promoting ethical action through democratic dialogue. *Change, 35*(5), 14–17.

Marchel, C. A. (2004). Evaluating reflection and sociocultural awareness in service-learning classes. *Teaching of Psychology, 31*(2), 120–123.

Markus, G., Howard, J., & King, D. (1993). Integrating community service and classroom instruction enhances learning: Results from an experiment. *Educational Evaluation and Policy Analysis, 15,* 410–419.

Mill, J. S. (1939). On liberty. In E. A. Burtt (Ed.), *The English philosophers from Bacon to Mill* (pp. 949–1041). New York, NY: Random House. (Original work published 1859)

Morgan, W., & Streb, M. (2001). Building citizenship: How student voice in service-learning develops civic values. *Social Science Quarterly, 82*(1), 154–169.

Murray, H., Gillese, E., Lennon, M., Mercer, P., & Robinson, M. (1996). Ethical principles for college and university teaching. In L. Fisch (Ed.), *New directions for teaching and learning: No. 66. Ethical dimensions of college and university teaching: Understanding and honoring the special relationship between teachers and students* (pp. 57–63). San Francisco, CA: Jossey-Bass.

Myers-Lipton, S. J. (1996). Effect of a comprehensive service-learning program on college students' level of modern racism. *Michigan Journal of Community Service-Learning, 3,* 44–54.

National Association for the Education of Young Children. (1998). *Code of ethical conduct.* Retrieved December 17, 2004, from http://www.naeyc.org/about/positions/PSETH98.asp

National Association of Social Workers. (1999). *Code of ethics.* Retrieved December 15, 2004, from www.socialworkers.org/pubs/code/default.asp

National Organization for Human Service Education. (1996). *Ethical standards of human service professionals.* Retrieved December 16, 2004, from http://www.nohse.com/ethics.html

National Service-Learning Clearinghouse. (2001). *Educator's guide to service-learning program evaluation.* Retrieved December 16, 2004, from http://www.servicelearning.org/filemanager/download/37/

National Service-Learning Clearinghouse Library. (2003). *Risk management and liability in higher education service-learning.* Retrieved December 17, 2004, from http://www.servicelearning.org/article/archive/143/

National Society of Professional Engineers. (2003). *NSPE code of ethics for engineers.* Retrieved December 16, 2004, from http://www.nspe.org/ethics/eh1-code.asp

Nist, S. L., & Holschuh, J. P. (1999). *Active learning: Strategies for college success.* Upper Saddle River, NJ: Longman.

Noddings, N. (1984). *Caring: A feminist approach to ethics and moral education.* Berkeley, CA: University of California Press.

Oates, K. K., & Leavitt, L. H. (2003). *Service-learning and learning communities: Tools for integration and assessment.* Washington, DC: Association of American Colleges and Universities.

O'Grady, C. R. (Ed.). (2000). *Integrating service-learning and multicultural education in colleges and universities.* Mahwah, NJ: Lawrence Erlbaum.

Osborne, R. E., Hammerich, S., & Hensley, C. (1998). Student effects of service-learning: Tracking change across a semester. *Michigan Journal of Community Service-Learning, 5,* 5–13.

Pascarella, E. T., & Terenzini, P. T. (1991). *How college affects students: Findings and insights from twenty years of research.* San Francisco, CA: Jossey-Bass.

Policy Center on the First Year of College. (2002–2003). *Second National Survey of First-Year Academic Practices 2002.* Retrieved December 16, 2004, from http://www.brevard.edu/fyc/survey2002/findings.htm

Puka, D. (Ed.). (1994). *Moral development: A compendium* (Vol. 3). New York, NY: Garland.

Purtilo, R. (1999). *Ethical dimensions in the health professions* (3rd ed.). Philadelphia, PA: W. B. Saunders.

Rest, J. R. (1988). Why does college promote development in moral judgment? *Journal of Moral Education, 17*(3), 183–194.

Rest, J. R. (1990). *Guide for the defining issues test.* Minneapolis, MN: University of Minnesota Press.

Rest, J. R., Narvaez, D., Bebeau, M. J., & Thoma, S. (1999). *Postconventional moral thinking: A neo-Kohlbergian approach.* Mahwah, NJ: Lawrence Erlbaum.

Rossi, P. H., Freeman, H. E., & Lipsey, M. W. (1999) *Evaluation: A systematic approach* (6th ed.). Thousand Oaks, CA: Sage.

Saltmarsh, J. (1997). *New directions for student services.* San Francisco, CA: Jossey-Bass.

Sax, L. J., & Astin, A. W. (1997, Summer/Fall). The benefits of service: Evidence from undergraduates. *Educational Record, 78,* 25–32.

Schaffer, M. A., Paris, J. W., & Vogel, K. (2003). Ethical relationships in service-learning partnerships. In S. H. Billig & J. Eyler (Eds.), *Deconstructing service-learning: Research exploring context, participation, and impacts* (pp. 147–168). Greenwich, CT: Information Age.

Schneider, C. G. (2004). *Practicing liberal education: Formative themes in the re-invention of liberal learning.* Retrieved December 16, 2004, from http://www.aacu-edu.org/publications/pdfs/Practicing_Liberal _Education.pdf

Shavelson R. J., & Huang, L. (2003, January/February). Responding responsibly to the frenzy to assess learning in higher education. *Change, 35*(1), 10–19.

Sigmon, R. (1994). *Linking service-learning with learning in liberal arts education.* Washington, DC: Council of Independent Colleges.

Snow, D. L., Grady, K., & Goyette-Ewing, M. (2000). A perspective on ethical issues in community psychology. In J. Rappaport & E. Seidman (Eds.), *Handbook of community psychology* (pp. 897–917). New York, NY: Kluwer/Plenum.

Stamm, L. (2004). Can we bring spirituality back to campus? Higher education's re-engagement with values and spirituality. *Journal of College and Character, 2.* Retrieved December 16, 2004, from http:// www.collegevalues.org/articles.cfm?a=1&id=1075

Stoddard, E. W., & Cornwell, G. H. (2003, Summe r). Peripheral visions: Towards a geoethics of citizenship. *Liberal Education, 89*(3), 44–51.

Strage, A. A. (2000). Service-learning: Enhancing student outcomes in a college-level lecture course. *Michigan Journal of Community Service-Learning, 7,* 5–13.

Tellez, K. (2000). Reconciling service learning and the moral obligations of the professor. In C. R. O'Grady (Ed.), *Integrating service-learning and multicultural education in colleges and universities* (pp. 71–92). Mahwah, NJ: Lawrence Erlbaum.

Troppe, M. (Ed.). (1995). *Connecting cognition and action: Evaluation of student performance in service learning courses.* Denver, CO: Education Commission of the States/Campus Compact.

Valerius, L., & Hamilton, M. L. (2001). The community classroom: Serving to learn and learning to serve. *College Student Journal, 35*(3), 339–345.

Vogelgesang, L. J., & Astin, A. W. (2000). Comparing the effects of service-learning and community service. *Michigan Journal of Community Service-Learning, 7,* 25–34.

Volbrecht, R. M. (2002). *Nursing ethics: Communities in dialog.* Upper Saddle River, NJ: Prentice Hall.

Weithorn, L. A. (1987). Informed consent for prevention research involving children: Legal and ethical issues. In J. A. Steinberg & M. M. Silverman (Eds.), *Preventing mental disorders: A research perspective* (pp. 226–242). Rockville, MD: U.S. Department of Health and Human Services.

Young, R. (1997). *No neutral ground: Standing by the values we prize in higher education.* San Francisco, CA: Jossey-Bass.

Zlotkowski, E. (1996, January/February). Linking service learning and the academy: A new voice at the table? *Change, 28*(1), 20–28.

Zlotkowski, E. (Ed.). (1997–2002). *Service-learning in the disciplines.* Washington, DC: American Association for Higher Education.

Zlotkowski, E. (Ed.). (1998). *Successful service-learning programs: New models of excellence in higher education.* Bolton, MA: Anker.

Index